ADVANCED
BADMINTON

PHYSICAL EDUCATION ACTIVITIES SERIES

Consulting Editor:
AILEENE LOCKHART
University of Southern California
Los Angeles, California

Evaluation Materials Editor:
JANE A. MOTT
Smith College
Northampton, Massachusetts

ARCHERY, Wayne C. McKinney
BADMINTON, Margaret Varner Bloss
BADMINTON, ADVANCED, Wynn Rogers
BASKETBALL FOR MEN, Glenn Wilkes
BASKETBALL FOR WOMEN, Frances Schaafsma
BIOPHYSICAL VALUES OF MUSCULAR ACTIVITY, E. C. Davis,
    Gene A. Logan, and Wayne C. McKinney
BOWLING, Joan Martin
CANOEING AND SAILING, Linda Vaughn and Richard Stratton
CIRCUIT TRAINING, Robert P. Sorani
CONDITIONING AND BASIC MOVEMENT CONCEPTS, Jane A. Mott
CONTEMPORARY SQUARE DANCE, Patricia A. Phillips
FENCING, Muriel Bower and Torao Mori
FIELD HOCKEY, Anne Delano
FIGURE SKATING, Marion Proctor
FOLK DANCE, Lois Ellfeldt
GOLF, Virginia L. Nance and E. C. Davis
GYMNASTICS FOR MEN, A. Bruce Frederick
GYMNASTICS FOR WOMEN, A. Bruce Frederick
HANDBALL, Michael Yessis
ICE HOCKEY, Don Hayes
JUDO, Daeshik Kim
KARATE AND PERSONAL DEFENSE, Daeshik Kim and Tom Leland
LACROSSE FOR GIRLS AND WOMEN, Anne Delano
MODERN DANCE, Esther E. Pease
RACQUETBALL/PADDLEBALL, Philip E. Allsen and Alan Witbeck
PHYSICAL AND PHYSIOLOGICAL CONDITIONING FOR MEN, Benjamin Ricci
RUGBY, J. Gavin Reid
SKIING, Clayne Jensen and Karl Tucker
SKIN AND SCUBA DIVING, Albert A. Tillman
SOCCER, Richard L. Nelson
SOCCER AND SPEEDBALL FOR WOMEN, Jane A. Mott
SOCIAL DANCE, William F. Pillich
SOFTBALL, Marian E. Kneer and Charles L. McCord
SQUASH RACQUETS, Margaret Varner Bloss and Norman Bramall
SWIMMING, Betty J. Vickers and William J. Vincent
SWIMMING, ADVANCED, James A. Gaughran
TABLE TENNIS, Margaret Varner Bloss and J. R. Harrison
TAP DANCE, Barbara Nash
TENNIS, Joan Johnson and Paul Xanthos
TENNIS, ADVANCED, Chet Murphy
TRACK AND FIELD, Kenneth E. Foreman and Virginia L. Husted
TRAMPOLINING, Jeff T. Hennessy
VOLLEYBALL, Glen H. Egstrom and Frances Schaafsma
WEIGHT TRAINING, Philip J. Rasch
WRESTLING, Arnold Umbach and Warren R. Johnson

PHYSICAL EDUCATION
ACTIVITIES SERIES

ADVANCED BADMINTON

WYNN ROGERS

*Player and Coach for United States
Thomas Cup Teams, 1949-1968
Arcadia, California*

WM. C. BROWN COMPANY PUBLISHERS
DUBUQUE, IOWA

Printed in the United States of America

Preface

This book assumes that its reader has already learned to play a good basic game of badminton. It is written not for the beginner but rather for the person who is well-started and highly motivated to become an advanced or expert badminton player. The reader will find many points which are not available in other books. Few competitors will talk much about what they have learned, for competitors want to win. A player gains his information about advanced play by observing and playing against the better players of all types over a period of years. As the result of experience he develops his particular technique and strategy. He learns what is effective by experimentation.

The author, Mr. Wynn Rogers, has been connected with *every United States Thomas Cup team*, either as a player or as a coach. He holds 25 national doubles championships (1947-present) and is acknowledged to be one of the best doubles players in the world. He is also a teacher, and in these pages Mr. Rogers shares what he has learned about the subtleties of the challenging and demanding sport of badminton. Here he reveals what tournament players know but what those who aspire to become fine players do not yet understand. Mr. Rogers does not explain any one style of play or any one set of idiosyncracies. Here are general, basic principles of fine play.

This book is not simple to read. It is "tight." It will be necessary to read and re-read, to practice and then re-read again. Mr. Rogers expresses these concepts in the words that are used and understood by top-class players, but the context in which they are used is completely understandable because these words are explained as they are introduced.

Self-evaluation questions are distributed throughout the text. These afford the reader typical examples af the kinds of understanding and levels of skill that he should be acquiring as he progresses toward mastery of advanced badminton. The player should not only answer the printed questions but should pose additional ones as a self-check on learning. Since the order in which the content of the text is read and the teaching progression of the instructor are matters of individual decision, the evaluative materials are not positioned according to the presentation of given topics. In some instances the student may find that he cannot respond fully and accurately to a question until he has read more extensively or has gained more playing experience. From time to time he should return to such troublesome questions until he is sure of the answers or has developed the skills called for, as the case may be.

Although this book was written primarily for college students enrolled in intermediate and advanced classes, the information is clearly suitable for and highly useful to anyone who aspires to be an above-average player or who hopes to appreciate tournament performance.

Aileene Lockhart

Contents

Fundamentals Reviewed

Varner has excellently described the basic fundamentals of the game in her book, *Badminton* (William C. Brown Company Publishers.) Here we concentrate on playing at the more advanced level. This book is written for the student who aspires to play well and for the tournament player who is anxious to play better. However, it seems wise to reemphasize a few basics that are sometimes forgotten or overlooked, even by champions.

It behooves anyone who wishes to become an advanced player to keep in mind that the fundamentals cannot be overlooked. Eager to be successful, the novice may choose to use any method or device that gets results now. Because he achieves temporary success (against inferior competition) he may then continue his unsound technique for so long that it becomes virtually impossible to correct it. Neuromuscular coordination is achieved and skill is developed through numerous repetitions. Many players think, therefore, that if they spend many, many hours on the court, they will automatically improve. Though hours of practice should result in some achievement, it should be remembered that practice does not *necessarily* make perfection. Practicing properly, however, will make it possible for a player to get much closer to that goal.

There are three important fundamentals which even the champion sometimes forgets, and when he does he loses his effectiveness. First and probably most important is *getting the body behind the bird on all shots* and *transferring the weight from the back foot onto the front foot* as the shuttlecock is hit. Obviously, when your opponent fools you, it is not always possible to hit the bird in front of you. However, quite often one sees players, even in tournaments, with ample time to do this but who, through ignorance, tiredness, or plain laziness, fail to follow this one basic tenet of any racket sport. If this principle is followed, not only will the shot more likely be successful but, almost as important, the player will be able to

1

get back to his base of operations more quickly, thus less likely to be caught out of position by his opponent's next return.

The second important fundamental is to *hit the bird with the racket head at right angles to the bird* (i.e., with a flat surface). This is absolutely necessary when maximum power is needed, and particularly in the backhand clear, the smash and the drive. Any tilting of the racket sideways on smashes and clears or tilting forward or backward on drives means that the bird will not receive the full force of the racket head, therefore obviously detracting from the ultimate power possible.

The third fundamental, more often violated by the beginner but occasionally also by the tournament player, is to *contact the bird high*. Too many allow the bird to drop down to about head height before hitting it. The higher you contact the bird, the more effective your shot can be. From a high point you can smash, clear or hit a drop shot, and each will get to its destination much more quickly. From the lower point, the smash and the drop shot are considerably less effective because they must travel more outward toward your opponent. (Fig. 1, B2, 3) When not hit high, the

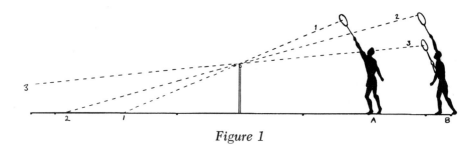

Figure 1

clear also takes longer to get to its destination because the bird must travel back upward to the height where it *should* have been contacted if it is to get over and, hopefully, behind your opponent. The more time you allow your opponent to recover and position himself, the less effective will be your shot. The word "time" as used here refers to *split seconds*.

2

2

Singles—
Styles and Strokes

STYLES

There are basically two types of singles players. One is the superbly conditioned athlete who relies almost entirely upon his quick reflexes and stamina to get back everything his opponent hits at him. This is the basically defensive player who plays every shot with as much safety as his opponent's returns allow. This player counts on the fact that as the match proceeds, his opponent will get progressively more tired and impatient, and consequently will make more and more errors.

The other type of player is the shot-maker who by accuracy, variety, and deception either wins the rally outright or, after a series of shots, forces a weak return from his opponent which can be put away by a smash or a quick drop. There have been men and women champions who have played both styles.

Which is the better? The aspiring player must realize that style is often dictated by physical and mental attributes and in part by climatic conditions. In the Orient, for example, one seldom sees the round-the-head shot used in singles because it is too enervating in the heat and humidity of these countries. Players there have developed excellent backhands so they need to take few steps and yet are still able to hit effectively. Whether the best defensive player of all time could beat the shot-maker of all time is obviously an academic question. If it were possible to match America's Dave Freeman, who played primarily defensively yet was considered by many to be the Babe Ruth of badminton, with either of the two great Danish shot-makers, Finn Kobbero or Erland Kops, with both contestants at their prime, then perhaps we could learn which style of play is the better. Perhaps somewhere in between lies the perfect singles player, i.e., one who has all the shots, deception, power and aggressiveness of the shot-maker, and the quickness, complete court coverage, endurance, and patience of the defensive player.

3

But to get to very practical concerns. The young player should decide early which type of stroke he will use on the upper left side of his body: the backhand or the round-the-head. Many steps, and consequently much energy, can be saved by developing a repertoire of offensive shots from the backhand side. The main advantage of the round-the-head is that it always poses the threat of a powerful smash, whereas the backhand smash, not being so powerful, is usually successful only once or twice during a match and then only because of its surprise effect.

After the decision is made, then that stroke should be practiced exclusively until it is completely mastered. One word of caution. Many young players think that after having developed a good versatile backhand, they no longer have to move so quickly nor get their bodies behind the bird—they need only to reach behind them. This is wrong. The only time the champs do this is when they have been fooled and so must do this to get out of trouble, or when they wish to pace themselves.

The young player should not only work to achieve control and accuracy of his shots in practice games but also must not be afraid to *use* these shots in a tournament. Often a player, in his desire to win present matches, will revert to an undesirable technique and consequently will delay his complete mastery of the proper shot. Assuming that a player has, however, achieved at least a partial mastery of a shot, then a *very* large factor in its successful execution is *concentration* and having the *confidence* that he will execute it as desired. If a shot is missed, the blame can be laid to some mechanical error such as improper body positioning or grip, but more often to lack of concentration or confidence. Occasionally of course a shot is missed due to over-eagerness—this is far more understandable and excusable than the other reasons. If a match is so important that winning is more important than mastering shots, perhaps the following technique could be used as a compromise. Since your opponent does not earn a point if he wins a rally that you have served, then "practice" during this rally, using it as the time when you try to make a finer shot, or as the time when you take a calculated risk on surprising him with an unusual tactic that might normally be a little risky. By the same reasoning, take no chances when your opponent is serving—when he serves, play your shots safer, be patient and, if necessary, play a little more defensively.

STROKES

If there is any one skill more important than any other to a singles player, it is the ability to camouflage his shots, thus not tipping off to his opponent which shot is coming. *Camouflage must be the first goal* a player should concentrate on as he develops *each* shot. If he waits until he has already developed the basic shots before he attempts to master the deception that is needed he will experience great difficulty in changing habits that have been built.

4

Due to the shape of the court, the drop and the clear are most frequently used in singles, the ultimate purpose being either to win the rally outright with a well concealed, well angled, quick drop shot to the floor or to force a weak return of the quick drop or attacking clear, either of which can then be put away with the smash. Consequently, the three basic singles shots—the smash, the drop shot, and the fast clear *must* be executed with the same preparatory movement of the arm and body.

THE SMASH. Pattern your attacking clear and drop shot from your smash. There are three basic parts to the smash: (1) the back-swing, coupled with the upward, then forward movement of the arm; (2) the uncocking of the forearm; and (3) the uncocking of the wrist. To obtain ultimate power in the smash, a full, sweeping back-swing, like that of a powerful tennis serve, is required. As the upper arm is brought upward and forward, the forearm and wrist are cocked back, with the elbow bent and leading the forearm momentarily in order to get a whipping action of the forearm as it straightens. The final part occurs a fraction of a second later, as the wrist uncocks and adds the impetus to the smash. The secret is coordination and *timing*. If any one of the basic parts of the smash is not coordinated rhythmically with the other two, the total movement will be disjointed and power will be lost. The forearm and wrist movements must be timed so the bird is met approximately one foot ahead of the forward foot and in line with the right shoulder; this must occur at the *precise* moment that the final part of the smash is culminated, that is, as the wrist is snapped. If the swing is delayed so the bird is met at any place later than the proper point, the hitter cannot utilize either the full force of his arm swing or the complete uncocking of his forearm and wrist. Nor can he hit the bird at the proper downward angle.

To be totally effective, the smash should be angled sharply downward so it just misses the net on its way to the floor. The closer to the floor your opponent must hit any of your shots, the more time you will have to recover to your own base of operations. Because of the sharp downward angle of your smash, he will also be forced to play closer to the net, thus making your attacking clear that much more effective. There are some top-notch singles players, however, who do not attempt to angle their smashes sharply downward because they feel that, if used properly (i.e., when the opponent has been out-maneuvered), angle is not as important as speed. This latter type of smash does have one important factor in its favor—it is not necessary to hit it so close to the net and therefore you have a much higher margin of safety.

The flat or outward smash is also effective when your opponent has misjudged or mis-hit a quick clear as a reply to your drop shot, and consequently has hit it low enough for you to intercept it. You can then hit it past him before he can get back to the center of the court. One word of caution: there are some players who, as beginners, felt it was necessary

Which two complementary shots should be used with your two overhead crosscourt drop shots?

Evaluation Questions

to bend backward almost double in order to get more "back" into their smashes. It is true that when the body acts as a whip, it will produce additional power to a smash. However, if this is done with the smash then the emphasized movement of the back must also be used during the execution of each drop shot and fast clear, otherwise the player will telegraph his intentions. Since the smash is used much less in singles than are the two other basic shots, the extra energy expended by this back movement is not justified. The little extra speed that is gained is not worth the cost.

Players sometimes overuse the smash. This practice can be very tiring, especially over the period of time required by the many matches which must be played during a tournament. The smash should be used either as the *coup-de-grace* after a series of shots has produced a weak return, or as an occasional surprise. Never should a smash be hit when you have to leap off the floor and are going backward at the same time. The odds are too great against even getting the bird in the court and, even if you should, you make yourself too vulnerable to the drop shot which your opponent may place just over the net. You cannot go anywhere while you are in the air. As in all shots, the body should be behind the bird when smashing and the weight should be transferred from the back onto the front foot as contact is made. Not only will the smash have a greater chance of success because of the good body balance so achieved, but as the shot is being made, you will be moving back toward your base of operations and will thereby be less likely to be caught out of position.

THE DROP SHOT. There are six overhead strokes that originate from the baseline which are generally known as drop shots. There are other shots that are also classified as drops (i.e., a drop as a reply to a smash or a drive, and a drop as a reply to a drop, often called *net shots*). All these are referred to below as drops, unless specifically noted otherwise. The six overhead drop shots are: (1) *the overhead forehand drop* straight ahead, and (2) crosscourt; (3) *the round-the-head drop* straight ahead and (4) crosscourt; and (5) *the overhead backhand drop* straight ahead and (6) crosscourt. (Note: all explanations assume the reader is right-handed.) Of these strokes, most players—even champions—have found it necessary to master only two or three. It is far better to *master* two or three drop shots than to try to partially execute all six. The following combinations are suggested, depending upon what style the player has decided to use. If he has decided to develop his backhand to as great a degree as his forehand, (therefore never using the round-the-head stroke in singles), then the combination of 2 and 6 are the best to master. The two best complementary clears to use with this combination are the straight ahead clears off both wings. If, on the other hand, the player has decided to use the round-the-head stroke whenever possible, instead of the backhand, then the combination of 2 and 4 drop shots are the best. After these two have been mastered, 1 is the next most useful drop.

There are two types of drop shots. The *fast drop* travels more in a forward direction but is quicker, much like that of a well-angled smash, and must, of necessity, go a little deeper into the opponent's court because of the speed with which it is hit. The *slow drop* is hit in such a way that it has almost completely lost all forward speed as it reaches the net, and it falls, ideally, almost straight downward after passing the net. The slow drop is not very popular now because so many players are very quick. Its relative slowness lessens its effectiveness both from the standpoint of winning the rally out right, or of setting up a winning shot. About the only time it should be used is when you have been caught out of position and need time to recover to your base. Even then, a clear is less dangerous and gives you more time to recover.

Two of the three straight ahead drop shots, 3 and 5, are not as effective or as useful as the others, so are not discussed here except in a supplementary manner.

The *round-the-head crosscourt drop* is hit downward with the same preparatory movement of the arm and body as used in the smash. (Figure 2A) However, instead of coming straight through with a flat racket, as in the smash, the racket is brought across the rear and left side of the bird in a circular or sideward motion to the left *as well as* in a forward and downward direction. The body, arm and racket head must get behind and to the left of the bird so that the sideward motion of the racket on the follow-through can be executed, and so that the bird can be directed to your right. (Most players end up with the follow-through to the right of the body but far more deception is possible when the follow-through is to the left, for example in Joe Alston's most effective drop.) (Figure 2A)

To hit a *forehand crosscourt fast drop* to your left, the racket face is tilted slightly to the left, and the bird is contacted slightly to its right but

7

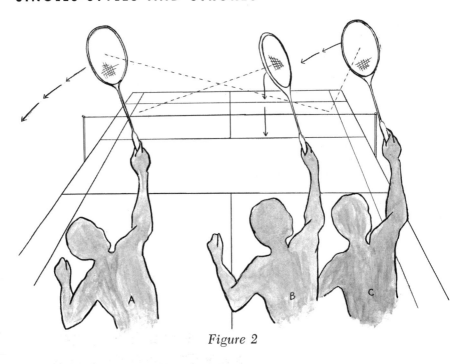

Figure 2

mostly to its rear at a downward angle, much like the slice serve in tennis. You must hit *through* the bird in a downward direction. (Figure 2B) The amount that the racket is tilted to the left determines how far sideways the bird will go, (i.e., if the bird is contacted from near your right sideline, the racket must be tilted more to the left in order to hit the bird to the extreme left sideline than would be the case if the bird is hit from the middle of the court).

The *overhead backhand crosscourt dropshot* is very similar to, and executed like, the forehand slice drop shot, except that it goes from left to right. The racket is tilted to the right and is drawn across the bird and downward to the right.

The third most effective drop, the *overhead forehand drop straight ahead,* is executed similarly to the round-the-head-crosscourt drop, the difference being that the bird is contacted directly at its rear rather than at the left rear. (Figure 2C). In *both* the round-the-head crosscourt and the forehand straight ahead drops, it is imperative to accentuate the circular action of the arm and racket sideways to the left on the follow through. This motion temporarily immobilizes your opponent or causes him to shift his weight in the direction of the racket and away from the drop. However you should be cautioned not to overemphasize this circular motion to the

8

Evaluation Questions

Can you hit seven out of ten attacking clears that land between the back doubles service line and the baseline? eight out of ten? nine out of ten?

extent that the bird is overly slowed down. Hit *through* the bird and downward so it travels to the floor. Care must be taken *not* to tip off your shot by starting this circular motion too soon. It should be started as the forearm uncocks.

THE CLEAR. There are two main types of clears: the offensive kind, known variously as the attacking, fast, or quick clear; and the defensive type, sometimes called the high clear. The latter is normally hit with an underhand stroke, forehand or backhand, from close to the floor. Usually it is hit as a direct result of your opponent's deceptive shot. It is obviously the less desirable of the two for you give your opponent more time to do as he pleases. This stroke is hit upward, high and deep, so as to land near your opponent's baseline. This gives you more time to recover in case you must scramble for your opponent's last shot.

The fast clear from the overhead forehand side is hit with the same preparatory arm and body motions which you use in the overhead forehand smash and drop shot. But the bird is hit a little later and is hit primarily in an outward and forward direction, high enough so your opponent cannot intercept it before it gets near his baseline. It is either hit with a flat racket or is sliced somewhat, and is hit hard enough to get behind your opponent though obviously not beyond his baseline. When hit with a *flat* racket, you will have to restrict the follow-through of your wrist in order to keep the bird in the court. This is not as deceptive a clear as when the bird is *slightly* cut or the circular action of the straight ahead drop is used, because most players unconsciously ease up slightly at some point in the forward arm swing instead of letting up on the wrist action. When either the slice or circular method is used, the player must take as full a swing on his clear as on his smash in order to make the bird go the length of the court, thus adding more deception.

9

The round-the-head fast clear should be hit with the same action as the round-the-head quick drop but it is hit outward instead of angled steeply downward, and with more force. To be fully effective, it should be executed with the same circular racket action as in the round-the-head crosscourt drop.

How high above the floor your clear should travel varies with each opponent. It will obviously have to travel in a higher plane for a taller player and for a leaper. Some short players can leap very high and intercept what appears to be an adequate high clear. If your opponent is allowed to intercept, he not only does not have to run as far, but he also has the added advantage of being able to send his next shot to its intended destination sooner, thereby increasing the risk that you will be caught out of position.

THE FLICK CLEAR. Somewhere in between the fast clear and the defensive clear is the flick clear. This is hit primarily with a quick uncocking or snapping of the wrist in an underhand stroke and in an upward and forward direction. It is hit from between the knees and the chest, depending upon how soon you can get to the bird. The flick clear is basically offensive, even though hit from a defensive spot. Its purpose is to attempt to nullify whatever advantage your opponent may have gained from his previous downward shot. If mixed with a well disguised drop shot, this can be an effective stroke with which to neutralize an opponent's offensive shot and possibly it can even turn the control of the rally around to you. The accuracy of your judgment in determining how low you can hit this shot safely is all important. Since it is usually used as a return of a drop shot, your opponent will smash it away if you hit it too low. If you hit it too high, he will have more time to recover and you will allow him to keep control of the rally.

If you should flick clear every time your opponent drops, he would control you too much, and you would end up doing most of the running while he "lays back" waiting for your clears. Therefore it is essential to develop a drop which you can use as a reply to your opponent's overhead drop, one which either immobilizes him or, better yet, makes him move backward. The crosscourt drop executed with either the forehand or backhand from near the net is most frequently used to achieve this objective. The sooner you get to his drop, the more effective will be *your* drop. Move quickly toward the bird and use a quick sideward stroke of the arm with the racket traveling almost parallel with the net, though tilted backward in order to undercut or slice the bird. Slicing in this case is necessary in order to keep the bird from going out of court. This stroke can be executed with or without wrist action. The latter is recommended because with it you can show your opponent more action, thus probably causing him to "freeze." This action when coupled with quick forward body movement gives your opponent the momentary impression that you are rushing the net, and thus causes him to hesitate. By the time he recovers, the bird should be on the floor or very close to it.

Another variation of the crosscourt drop is used when you have been able to contact his drop at approximately net level and he is aware that you *could* punch a drive at him. Come in fast with a lunge, forearm and wrist cocked straight in front of you, racket flat as if to punch the bird. However, as the forearm extends, the wrist turns the racket sideways thus slicing the bird toward the furthest alley. This shot will be far more effective if, earlier in the match, you had punched a drive at him. A smart player, of course, will not be fooled long if you always do the same thing.

Photo 1

Another type of drop that should be mastered by the complete player is the *straight up and down or hair-pin drop.* Although this is very useful against all types of players, it is absolutely necessary against a strictly defensive player, particularly if your shots have not been very effective in out-maneuvering him because of his great speed and retrieving ability. It is also very useful for obtaining a weak clear in doubles play. This drop is hit upward with an open racket, softly so as to go straight up, just clearing the net, and falling, ideally, within one to three inches of the net on his

11

side. The purpose is to force him to contact the bird as low and as close to the net as possible, forcing him to hit either a very short clear or to re-drop. Proximity to the net is far more vital in obtaining a short clear than the height at which he contacts the bird, assuming that he contacts it at least a foot below the net. (Photo #1)

You must have made obvious the threat of a flick clear prior to executing this drop in order to keep your opponent back, otherwise he will move in and meet the bird within a few inches of the top of the net. The wrist, therefore, must be slightly cocked and, ideally, the body should be slightly to one side of the bird. If the bird is contacted straight out in front of your right shoulder with a flat racket, your flick clear will tend to go upward and too high and, if that happens, the offense is lost. This is particularly true of a forehand flick.

It is *imperative*, after seeing that you have hit a good close drop and that your opponent must contact it at least a foot below the net on his side, for you not to be taken in by any fake he might use to drive you back from the net. Move in and be ready to "kill" any return drop that might be a few inches too high. Should he clear, it cannot be any farther back than halfway, allowing you ample time to get back and smash it away for a winner.

Another valuable drop by which singles players can force a weak clear or an outright error is the undercut drop, discussed in Chapter 3, "The Netman's Role." The opportunity to use it occurs more frequently in doubles since it is more easily executed as a reply to an opponent's drop which originates from around the net.

THE SERVE. The high, deep serve is customarily used in singles play. It should travel forward and upward to a height of between 20-25 feet, ending its forward motion, or peak, just over your opponent's baseline. At this point the bird falls straight down, thus presenting your opponent a relatively "dead" bird to hit. Be sure to take your stance each time at the same spot on the court for otherwise you will never achieve a uniform or reliable serve.

Depth to your opponent's baseline is *very* important in the high serve. If you serve short, not only will you give him the opportunity to get his quick clears behind you sooner but also his smash can get to its mark quicker; furthermore, you will give him a steeper angle for both his smash and drop. Add to this the fact that he will not have to go as far to his base after his return, and you will quickly recognize that you are giving away a considerable edge when you serve short. (See Fig. 1-A1, P. 2.)

First, assume a wide but comfortable stance so your weight can be easily transferred from one foot to the other. Next, bring the arm back in a full arc as the bird is dropped approximately a foot *ahead* of the left foot but in line with your right shoulder. As the arm is brought forward, the wrist should be cocked back, the body weight being transferred from

Evaluation Questions

What is the basic tenet for getting and keeping control of a rally?

the right to the left foot as the arm comes upward with a full easy swing. The uncocking of the wrist, if timed properly and if hit with a flat racket, should give ample impetus to the bird so that it will achieve proper height and depth without your having to strain or force your stroke. The bird must be met in front of the body, otherwise it will go too much upward and not deep enough. The arm should be brought forward in a straight line past the hip, with the follow-through of the racket head above and to the left of your head.

One word of caution in learning the high singles serve: it is a very natural thing to want to take a short step with the left foot as you start the forward movement of your arm. The rules prohibit this and it can be a very difficult habit to break if allowed to become ingrained. It can also be very upsetting when called by an umpire at a crucial point in a match.

When playing an opponent whose best shots are very effective overhead drops and clears and who has caused you a lot of trouble with his return of your high serve, it would be advisable to try the low serve as possibly an easier and surer method of gaining points. This is executed like the low doubles serve except that you take your stance a little deeper in the court than you would in doubles—so you can defend against a flick clear.

There are also the other two predominantly doubles serves, the drive and the flick. These are discussed in the chapter on doubles. If these serves can be used advantageously in singles, it would of course be wise to do so.

RETURN OF SERVE. Since the rules of badminton force the server to hit upwards, and since the majority of singles serves are high, as the receiver you *must* develop the two main means of returning the high serve—

13

What can you tell about the length of your clears and serves when your opponent's feet are in each of these three positions as he makes the return?

Evaluation Questions

CHECKING YOUR CLEARS AND SERVES

the *attacking clear* and the *fast drop* from both sides of the court—to such a degree of accuracy and deception that you do not relinquish control. If and when you do lose control, your opponent stands a good chance of winning a point.

When receiving a high serve to your right court, use: the forehand straight ahead fast clear to his backhand, mixed with either the forehand sliced cross-court fast drop or the quick forehand drop straight ahead.

When receiving a high serve to your left court, use: the round-the-head cross-court quick drop mixed with the fast clear straight ahead to his forehand. You can add to these two returns another pair that can keep your opponent on his toes: the round-the-head smash straight ahead and crosscourt clear to his backhand, but use these sparingly because the smash can be tiring, and the crosscourt clear can be dangerous, if intercepted, because your opponent can deliver a smash to your forehand sideline before you can recover from your stroke.

When receiving a low serve in singles, get to the bird quickly and "hold" your shot with a cocked wrist for a fraction of a second, hoping to fake your opponent into thinking you intend to drop. Instead, the wrist is uncocked to flick clear. The companion shot to the flick is the drop executed from the same "holding" action. Keep the wrist cocked for this and, with a sudden movement of the forearm, tap it over. However, it is better to use a crosscourt drop with the slicing action described earlier if the bird can be contacted from a point near either *sideline*. There is too much risk of sending the bird out of court into the alley if this crosscourt drop is hit from near the middle of the court.

When receiving a drive serve, your reply will depend on whether you have been partially fooled or not. Since the drive serve customarily is used only to the backhand, the usual reply is to counter-drive *downward* toward

14

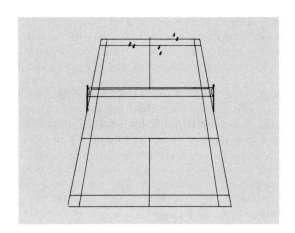

Diagram A:

CHECKING YOUR
CLEARS AND SERVES

the left or to drive clear to your opponent's backhand if you can get your racket around to meet the bird in front of you. A good variation to use in conjunction with your counter-drive and clear is a drop to either side with a full arm movement that is suddenly blocked on contact.

Your reply to the flick serve will be the same as that for the high serve. If it is short or low enough so you can intercept it, smash to either sideline. If it is deep, then clear or drop.

GENERAL TIPS AND STRATEGY

1. *Always* attempt to *get to all shots*, but especially to drop shots, as *quickly* as possible. You have much more choice when you meet the bird at net level. You can also fake more when you get it high. *To meet the bird high is the most important basic tenet for getting and keeping control of any rally.*

2. Don't over-run a drop shot. It is better to stop one or two steps short and reach to hit the bird than to go all the way and, as a result, be late in getting back to your base of operations. You can save many steps by doing this and also prevent cramping your strokes.

3. Your base of operations should be a little farther forward than the exact center of the court from net to baseline. It takes less time for the fast drop to get to its destination than does a fast clear. Conversely, you have more time to get back for a clear since the bird travels farther on a clear. Move in even closer to the net when your opponent is about to return your drop, assuming that you have made a good close drop. Your base from sideline to sideline will also vary according to where your opponent contacts the bird. From his extreme right, a smash straight ahead will get to your backhand quickly. Therefore move over to your left about a full step. The same policy applies to the other side.

15

4. Always come back to your base after every shot. The only exceptions to this advice are: (a) When you are *positive* that, because of the effectiveness of your shot, your opponent can only make one shot; and (b) When your opponent tips you off regarding his intentions. Take advantage of this gift by moving to the intended spot *as* he hits. If you make your move *before* he hits, you will indicate to him that he is doing something to tip you off and he may then be able to correct the flaw. If you move *as* he hits, his eyes will be on the bird and therefore he will be less likely to see you move.

5. Under no circumstances should you move until the bird is actually hit; if you do, you will be faked out of position. Badminton is a very fast game and you must be still, with knees slightly bent, ready to move instantly in any direction, at the *moment* your opponent hits the bird. Some players develop the bad habit of slightly jumping or hopping as the opponent hits. Guard against this fault.

6. Pick out either the cork or the green band on the bird and concentrate on this when hitting. This practice will lessen the number of mis-hits which you make.

7. Never change a winning game. Always change a losing one *unless* you are *certain* that, even though losing at the moment, the tide will turn in your favor if you persevere. There are many factors that can turn a match in your favor. Perhaps your opponent will tire and therefore start missing those previously precise drops, or perhaps he will become discouraged when his "Sunday best" shots start coming back. A "bad call" by a linesman or umpire can completely demoralize some players.

8 Do not do anything which might antagonize your opponent. To do so not only is poor sportsmanship, but it can also backfire. Many a match has been won by an apparently beaten player when the apparent winner did something, such as showing off, which in turn caused the adrenalin of the presumedly beaten opponent to flow and so he determined that "this show-off isn't going to beat me!" Be a relentless competitor but never to the point that you will do *anything* to win.

9. As a young or beginning player, you will tend to be impatient and try to smash at the least little opening. Don't forget that most opponents will gladly let you have the few brilliant, off-balance smashes that hit the line as long as you miss two or three for every one you make. Patience is an integral part of the make-up of the complete player. Wait for the moment when you have out-manuevered your opponent and have a 90% plus chance before "putting it away."

10. When you have a match with an unknown player and have no knowledge of his style or best shots, try to scout him as he plays in the previous round of a tournament. Try to discover any actions or movements of any kind which can tip you off regarding which shot is coming next. If it is not possible to see him play beforehand then try to pick up these things while warming up with him before your match starts.

11. When warming up, it is best to do just that, not *practice* your favorite shots. If you show your opponent too much, your shots will not be as effective as they otherwise would be when the match starts.

12. Playing facilities vary from hall to hall. There are walls reasonably close to the baseline in most halls. When most of your play has been done under these conditions and then you play in an enormous hall, you will tend to hit both your high serve and clears considerably shorter than usual. To get proper depth during the warm-up period, check your opponent's feet just before he hits your clear. If they are near the doubles service line (2½ feet from the baseline) you are getting good depth. With practice, you can use this procedure occasionally during play, especially when you sense that your clears are short. (Diagram A.) Of course, lack of depth could *also* result because your clears are too low and consequently your opponent is merely intercepting your shots. In order to find the proper depth for your clears during a match, it is better to lose *one* rally by hitting the bird progressively deeper and deeper until your opponent lets it drop beyond the baseline than to hit short repeatedly thus giving him control of *all* the rallies.

Also check your high serve for depth *every* time you use it. You will have ample time to do this while it is falling if the serve goes over 20 feet in height and falls straight down, as it should. If your serve is achieving the right depth, your opponent's right foot should be out of court behind his baseline as he steps into your serve. (See Diagram A.)

13. A good technique for developing proper depth may be practiced with a friend. Follow the rule that if either of you allows a clear to fall and it does not land within the area between the doubles service line and the baseline, the hitter loses that rally.

14. Keep in mind that, during the course of many matches, you will benefit from approximately 50 percent of the mistakes made by linesmen and umpires. It seems to be human nature to remember only the bad calls! No player becomes a champion if he constantly lets bad calls affect his play. A display of temper can give your opponent confidence, and so make matters even worse for you.

15. Do not give your opponent "cheap" points on his serves. Play a trifle more conservatively if necessary to keep control of the rally. Every time you make an error, he moves another point closer toward match point. If you wish to gamble on a risky smash or a finely executed drop shot, do it during a rally that you have served so as not to give him a point.

16. If an opponent has so much overhead deception when returning your high serve that you have great difficulty just getting the bird in play, it might be wise to serve low to him. Sometimes this serve can get you a few points if he attempts too close a drop, or perhaps when you gamble that he will hit a flick clear and step back to intercept it. By serving low, you take away his favorite higher percentage returns of your high serve, and at least you will get the bird in play for more than one or two strokes.

17

17. The center court theory can be very effectively employed against certain players, especially those who hit overhead drops and crosscourt *net* shots with a high degree of accuracy and finesse from either sideline. In accordance with this theory, every clear and drop is hit right down the middle of the court. Not only does this placement cut down on the severity of the angle of the return but you will force these players to do quite a bit of adjusting; you will probably take away their favorite shots. Furthermore, you will also reduce your chances of hitting out of court.

18. From time to time you will play a "south paw." Be aware of this probability and remember that this player's backhand is to your *left*. Some players have been known to play a whole match without realizing that the opponent was left handed; consequently they played most of their shots to the opponent's stronger side.

19. The player who uses the round-the-head stroke rather than the backhand is vulnerable to a combination of drops to *his* forehand and clears to his backhand, because he must take an extra step or two backward in order to execute the round-the-head stroke. This combination of shots is easy to execute when stroking from your right side. However, a *quick* drop straight ahead from your left, whether from the round-the-head or the backhand, is very difficult to develop. Any such drop must of necessity be relatively slow. It would be better therefore to develop a well angled, controlled smash straight ahead from your left backcourt. This is tiring if used too frequently but can be mixed in a pattern with clears to either side.

20. When your opponent is flustered, don't allow him to do anything to change the pattern of his play. If a fast pace has been effective for you, don't let him slow it down, and vice versa. If you, however, are the one "on the run" then by all means attempt to change the pattern.

21. Some players play a fixed pattern of shots, perhaps alternating clears and drops, or two clears, then a drop, etc. Some always hit the smash or drop to the spot that you just came from when you have been caught out of position and are trying to get back to your base. Others always hit to the obvious opening. These little things may seem trivial but, if noted and the information used to your advantage, they can make a difference of many points during a match. Many matches are won by just one or two points. Obviously you must guard against forming such a pattern yourself.

22. There will be days when you don't have the usual touch. Shots that normally go in just miss. First of all, be honest in your evaluation. "Am I missing because my opponent's stroke production keeps me off balance"? If so, try anything to change the pattern. Perhaps slowing or speeding up the pace may help. If your opponent is particularly effective with a quick drop from one spot, don't hit to that spot. Serve low, with an occasional flick. Try the center court theory.

However if you are truly "off," try to play your shots a little safer, making sure that at least you keep the bird in play until things go right for you again. Under these conditions, the tendency is to become angry and frustrated which, of course, only tenses your muscles and causes more errors, especially on shots that require delicate touch and control. This often leads to loss of confidence in one or more of your shots. If you find that you are getting too tense, try a smash or two to relieve this tension and frustration. There is far less chance for error in a smash, providing you don't try to angle it too steeply, than in a quick drop.

23. Try to get a jump on your opponent at the *beginning* of the match by playing your shots a little safer and letting *him* make the errors. Some play better when ahead but "tie up" when behind. But some play better when behind, so don't think you automatically have the game won when you have a good lead. It seems to be human nature to "let up" under these circumstances and so you will have to guard against this tendency.

24. If your opponent has smashed straight ahead, your best bet is to hit a crosscourt drop, the farthest point away from your opponent. Using a short stroke, hit the bird with the racket angled toward the opposite front corner. If he has "beaten" you (so you cannot meet the bird in front of you), employ your wrist to a greater degree in order to hit the bird crosscourt.

If his smash is made crosscourt, attempt to block it straight ahead with a *locked* wrist but with a short quick upward movement of the arm, if there is time. This action will make him think you are hitting it back deep.

25. Sometimes your opponent, by his finely placed deceptive drop, causes you to scramble so much that you barely get to the bird. Don't make the mistake of hitting a flick clear because you need time to recover to your base. Instead, hit it very high and deep. Some players get desperate when they think they rightfully should have won a rally, and will start taking undue chances. Don't fall into the trap of impatience and recklessness.

26. Occasionally, you will run into a player who likes to hurry you when he is serving. He will serve the exact moment you come to a set position, but before you are crouched and mentally set. Don't hit his serve! The rules state that if you attempt to return it, you are considered ready. If you let it drop, make no effort to hit it and tell the umpire you were not ready, it must be re-served and no penalty is involved. Better solutions are to hold up your hand or to look down at the floor until you are ready. Of course, this advice should not be carried to the extreme of an unsportsman-like stall, but you *are* entitled to a reasonable amount of time in which to get set.

27. Pacing yourself can be a very important factor in a long, hard fought match. Excessive and improper smashing can be very tiring, and can leave you with very little energy toward the end of a long match, when it is vitally needed. But don't confuse pacing with "resting" or loafing—these lead to unnecessary errors. An example of pacing: You have won the first game but are far behind in the second. Attempt to run your opponent as much as possible while you relax. Sometimes by doing so, the finer, more closely hit shots which you previously were missing, will start to fall in

19

for winners. Above all, don't let your opponent make you do all the running. To prevent this, play your shots very close in an attempt to end the rallies quickly—one way or the other—so you will have something left for the third game, if required.

28. There are times when an all out effort may be worth the gamble. Assume that in the above situation you have closed the gap to 12-12, but you are getting very tired. An all out physical and mental effort to secure three points may not only win the match but save you the considerable effort of a third game.

29. Birds tend to speed up as much as a foot or more after they have been in play a while. If a regulation bird is more to your advantage than the faster one being used, you are entitled to, and should ask for, a new one (e.g., when you depend on overhead deception to get a quick clear *behind* your opponent but, because the bird has speeded up, your clears are going out beyond his baseline).

30. Occasionally, a slower hit shot by an opponent may be about to land close to the line but your feet block the linesman's vision so he cannot call the shot in or out. If it is out, you certainly don't want to have to play the rally over again when the point should have been yours. It isn't good sportsmanship to try to block the linesman's vision on a shot that is in. Develop the habit of stepping out of his line of vision whenever possible.

31. When you have won the toss and have the choice of serve or side, it may be advantageous to choose the side, particularly if one side of the court has a very bad background and visibility is much worse. In this case, choose the bad side for the first game so that if the match goes to three games, you will have the good side for the last and most important half of the third game.

32. When you reach 13 or 14 first and have the choice of setting or not setting the game to the maximum or minimum number of points, consider, before making your decision: (1) The relative tiredness of both players; (2) If it is the second game, which player won the first; (3) If one side has a poor background for visibility, which side you are on. Normally, if you feel you have the edge, choose the maximum allowed. At 14 all, particularly, you would really be gambling if you chose one or no set for he is serving and one lucky shot by him and you will have lost that game.

TRAINING. There is nothing which takes the place of actual play against an equal or better player. Not only do you strengthen all the muscle groups used in the sport but you more quickly master all the strokes. Of course, variety in competition is essential so learn to defend against all types of players. You can also adopt their more valuable shots and techniques.

The one valuable exercise is to skip rope. This is not only a great conditioner but it increases agility, an invaluable asset in badminton.

What do you do when you have developed to the point that you can quite easily beat the local players? Ask your instructor, if you are a student, for the address of the president of the local club and ask him about the procedure for joining. If this suggestion is not productive, write to Mrs. Virginia Lyon, Executive Secretary, American Badminton Association, 1330 Alexandria Drive, San Diego, California 92107. Better yet, organize your own club. Most public school Boards of Education are sympathetic and will allow the use of their facilities.

3

Men's and Women's Doubles

Men's and women's doubles utilize basically the same strokes, techniques, teamwork and strategy; therefore this discussion pertains to both. The few variations and differences between these games are discussed at the end of this chapter.

Although there have been some very fine doubles teams who consistently and deliberately played defensively and challenged all opponents to hit through them, none of today's top contestants play this style exclusively. It is rather well conceded that two of the better smashers will beat the better defensive players if they play a totally oriented defensive game. Consequently, *the most basic principle of all doubles play is to get the offensive and to keep it until the rally is won.* Therefore every shot should have, as its purpose, the ultimate goal of causing your opponents to lift the bird to you or your partner.

SYSTEM OF DOUBLES PLAY

Although there have been good doubles teams who have used other systems of play, all the better teams today use *the up and back system.* In this style of play both the server and the receiver are close to the net prior to the serve, and their respective partners are back. Which side then obtains the offense depends upon how good the serve is and how effectively the receiver returns it. When your team gains the offense, the smashing player is back and is responsible for all returns to the backcourt. The hitter's partner moves up somewhere near, or back of, the place where his front service line intersects the middle line. From here he is in a position to "kill" any weak return. When forced to give up the offense, then go into a side by side position, with each player responsible for his half of the court lengthwise. This is the best position from which to defend against your opponents' smashes.

Evaluation Questions

Can you deliver nine out of ten good, low doubles serves that land within three inches of the center and front service lines? flick serves within six inches of the back service line?

DOUBLES SERVES

THE LOW SERVE. In badminton, you do not make points unless your side served the rally just won. Consequently, if you expect to win points you must develop an accurate, low serve which just skims the net and lands near the intersection of the front service and mid-court lines. From this spot your opponent has less angle, thereby making his return of your serve more accessible to both you and your partner. Stand as close to the front service and mid-court lines as you can and still have control and confidence. Obviously, the farther your serve travels, the more time you give your opponent to rush it and to meet it while it is high, and thus make an offensive return. If your low serve accidentally is a little higher than it should be or if you deliberately hit a high serve, you give away the offense immediately.

Hold the bird out in front of the body with the forefinger and thumb of the left hand holding it at the top of the cork tip near where the quills enter the cork. The bird should be held so that the tip points straight down to the floor and should be released so that it *falls* straight down. If it is thrown or tossed, the bird tends to wobble and this causes inaccurate stroking. The arm and racket should be back as your stance is taken. When the bird is released, stroke the bird with a forward movement of the arm only. There is no time or necessity to take a backswing as the bird is dropped, as in the singles serve. The bird should be contacted as close to your waist as is legally allowed, so that it will not travel upward any more than necessary. *Ideally* the bird should reach its peak on *your* side of the net and be falling downward as it reaches the net.

The better players use various methods of serving. Some start with a short backswing, others use a fairly sweeping motion. Some contact the bird with a sideward slicing action, others relatively flat. Each method has

23

When X smashes to opponent O in doubles, is it generally best to aim to A, B, or C?

Evaluation Questions

AIMING
THE SMASH

its advantages and weaknesses. The sweeping motion makes a better flick possible because the bird is allowed to drop slightly and is hit with a flat racket. The sweeping motion suggests to your opponent that he should look for the flick—by the time he recovers, your serve is, ideally, below the level of the net on his side. The drive serve is possible to execute from this sweeping type of serve but it will be relatively weak because the bird is contacted from a lower point and consequently must be more upward when delivered.

The short backswing, requiring less motion, provides less chance for error. It is the best to use for the low and drive serves; but is less effective for the flick because of the lack of power in the short backswing.

Probably the best low serve to develop is one in which the racket is relatively flat on contact, with the wrist cocked back so that both the flick and drive serves can be effective alternatives (that is, by your movements you do not tip your opponent off regarding what is coming). The *arm* should be brought forward with the *same* speed on all serves, the uncocking of the wrist providing the last split second impetus to the bird when you drive or flick. The wrist remains cocked for the low serve, with the arm movement carrying the bird over the net.

THE DRIVE SERVE. The drive and flick serves are used to keep an opponent from crowding the net with rushing tactics, and should be used sparingly as a means of keeping your opponent "honest." These two serves go upward; you will give away the offense if you don't surprise him.

The drive serve is hit with great speed in as low a trajectory as the net allows and usually is sent to your opponent's backhand. The purpose is to "beat" him with the speed and unexpectedness of the shot—that is, you hope he will not have time to get his racket around to meet the bird out in front of him so he can hit an offensive smash or drive, or you hope

24

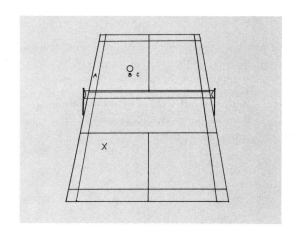

Diagram: B

AIMING
THE SMASH

to force him to make an outright error. This serve is more effective against a taller than a shorter player, since the former must bend his knees considerably in order to hit your drive from around his head or shoulders. To be fully effective, the drive serve should be hit from the same spot on your court as the low serve. If you deliver it from your regular front serving position, your opponent is not likely to reply with a drop shot. He probably will drive it back with his backhand or smash outward from around-the-head at you, the server. Since you have given away the offense with this serve, drop back a step or two as quickly as you can and anticipate a smash or drive. Should he drop, you are close enough to the net to get to the bird while it is still high. Some teams feel that the server should not drop back on a drive serve from his basic front position, but should move up and let his partner take the smash or drive since he is already back and has better body balance and position. The main disadvantage of this method is, since he is back farther, if and when the server's partner does return the drive or smash, he must contact the bird lower; therefore his return must be higher and thus more defensive. If the server, however, moves back and *does* get the drive or smash, he can make an offensive shot or, at worst, a fairly neutral, level drive.

Some players move back and over to the alley and use a drive serve, each doubles player then being responsible for his own side of the court lengthwise. This minimizes the downward angle of a round-the-head smash and at least gets the bird in play when the team has trouble getting its low serve to work against an effective rusher. This serve from your alley does make a lower drive possible since it is hit from farther back in the court. When this is done, however, there is no surprise element and all an experienced player has to do is drop shot or drive it downward with his backhand, follow it into the net, and you are then on the defensive. The occa-

25

Under what two common conditions is it advisable to use a drop
rather than a smash?

Evaluation Questions

sional use of an unusual shot or tactic can produce an error or weak return if your opponent has had little opportunity to practice it. If this serve is successful, it is best not to overdo it; save it for a critical point when a point is urgently needed.

A very effective team tactic when using the drive serve from the alley is for the server to move in quickly to the net, anticipating a drop, as the receiver contacts the serve. This is particularly effective when one or both opponents favor the drop rather than the drive as their return. The server's partner should be told or a pre-arranged signal given before each serve so that he knows his responsibilities.

If you have lost confidence in your low serve and must serve high in order to at least get the bird in play, it is better to serve a high singles type serve that comes straight down near the back service line rather than a flick serve. You will not only have more time to defend this type of serve, since it must be smashed from a spot deeper in the court, but also it is harder to smash for it is "dead" as it comes straight down. A better tactic under these circumstances, is to force your opponent to drop, by serving low from the sides position. With both you and your partner back in your respective halves of your court and ready for the drive or outward smash, the drop is the only logical reply. You then have two and one-half more feet for your clear than you would have for the high singles type serve.

THE FLICK SERVE. The flick serve follows the same principle as the flick clear. The purpose is to hit the bird just over your opponent's reach so that he cannot intercept it, even by leaping, and so that it falls behind him near his back service line. The preparatory arm movement is the same as that used in the low serve, with the wrist uncocking at the last split second. As with the drive serve, the flick should be used sparingly for if it is unsuccessful, your opponent will usually win the rally outright, or at least take the offense and ultimately win the rally. A flick serve, which can be very effective, is one that is sent to your opponent's alley or forehand when you are serving from your right court. It must travel as low as possible so it will not be intercepted, and be hit quickly so that he cannot "pull" it crosscourt. If it is not too high, he cannot smash downward at a sharp angle; this lets your partner expect the smash straight ahead to his backhand and reasonably high so that he can drive it back crosscourt past the netman and either win the point outright or obtain a weak return. If your serve has "beaten" your opponent, you will then be able to take any smashes to the middle and to the inside of your partner, thus relieving you of having to be prepared for a crosscourt smash to your forehand.

One word of caution. Many players work long hours to perfect the complete camouflaging of the low, drive, and flick serves so that no opponent can tell which serve is coming until the bird is actually hit. Yet they will give away their intentions with some little unobtrusive action such as looking at the spot to which they intend to serve. *Anything* that tips your opponent off (a look, a slightly different stance) must be guarded against.

ON THE OFFENSE

Once you get the bird up on your side in doubles, you basically have a choice of two shots, the smash or the overhead drop shot. The smash should be used predominantly, the purpose being to win the rally outright or to get a weak return which the net player can put away. However, there are times when the drop is more advisable. When your opponent is playing fairly well back in his court, a well concealed, quick drop can be a winner. Also when you are getting tired, a few drop shots can give you some respite as well as draw your opponent in closer to the net, thereby making your smash more effective. If he knows that you will always smash, however, he only has to prepare for one shot; he therefore can "lay back" away from the net and this gives him a better chance of returning your smash.

The one time that a drop is far more advisable than a smash is when your opponent has caught you off balance with a fast, low trajectory clear or a flick serve, thus making it impossible for you to get a good downward angle to your smash. If you smash under these circumstances, it will be an outward or flat smash, making it possible for your opponent to drive your smash back at net level to an unguarded spot or at least so low that you cannot smash again. If you use a drop shot first under these circumstances, you will then be on balance to smash his next clear which must be higher and more defensive.

All *smashing should be purposeful.* Just as important as speed are hitting to the proper spot, getting good downward angle, changing pace, and keeping both opponents on their toes.

Generally, the proper spot to aim your smash in doubles is to the inside (toward the mid-court line) of the opponent straight ahead of you.

27

Where is the most vulnerable spot at which to direct your smash against an opponent who defends with the backhand only, A, B, or C?

Evaluation Questions

SMASHING AGAINST
BACKHAND DEFENSE

(See Fig. 3C-D). His return, if successful, will in most cases, come right back to you. There are some players who can fall away sideways and guide the return of a smash crosscourt away from the smasher, but not consistently against a top smasher who has good downward angle *and* who mixes up the placement of his smashes.

Obviously, if you always hit to one spot your opponent can look for every smash there, thus simplifying his job considerably. An occasional

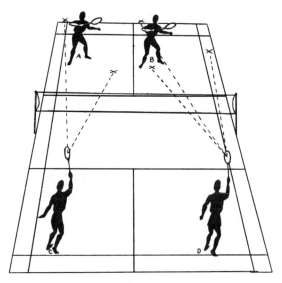

Figure 3

Diagram: C

SMASHING AGAINST
BACKHAND DEFENSE

smash down the alley straight ahead will keep him "honest." Your smash to the alley, however, *must* be all out in speed and must "beat" your opponent so that if he is able to get it back he will do so from a late swing—he won't be able to meet it out in front of him and thus drive it back crosscourt away from you. Probably the best *general* plan to follow is to hit to the inside of the man straight ahead with good downward angle until you get a fairly weak return from him; then use the alley or the other opponent for the "kill."

One advantage of smashing to the inside of the player straight ahead is that it gives your partner at the net knowledge about where the return will normally come, thus allowing him to anticipate and therefore put away many returns that he otherwise could not have.

Smashing to the opponent crosscourt from you can be dangerous if overdone, because his return can be hit back to the half court away from you. However, if he is reasonably sure that you never will smash at him, he can get considerable rest while you battle it out with his partner straight ahead of you. If he is to make an effective return of your smash or drop he must be constantly crouched, ready to move instantly on every shot whether it is to him or not. This can be very tiring. It is a good idea to smash crosscourt occasionally to keep both opponents alert; also possibly you may win the rally if the crosscourt smash is used sparingly. Make sure that you hit to his alley because most players protect the middle area first when they are crosscourt from the smasher. *Above all* make sure that you smash at a steep downward angle so that if he does get it back, the return will have to be fairly high, thus providing you with enough time to keep control of the rally.

Smashing down the middle can be effective occasionally, particularly against a "pick up" team which hasn't yet resolved the question of who

29

Can you place eight out of ten drop returns of the low serve so that the server must clear? nine out of ten? ten out of ten?

Evaluation Questions

should take what particular shot. However, it can be dangerous if you hit it by mistake to the opponent crosscourt from you, or if he is the one who normally takes the smash down the middle, since he can easily return it to the opposite side away from you. But you *can* smash to *any* spot on the court without getting into serious trouble and without losing control of the rally *if* you angle it steeply downward and *if* you are on balance when you hit. Under these conditions, any return must be fairly high, thus giving you time to move the width of the court, in which case you can either drop, if slightly off balance, or smash again. The smasher gets into trouble when he is not on balance, and when he attempts to smash a bird that is pushed at him at a height between his shoulders and head. It is impossible to get a good downward angle on such a smash for it *must* go more outward, or flat, than downward. (Fig. 1-B3, P. 2) It is this kind of a smash that can be leveled out by your opponent and driven back crosscourt just above the net for a winner, if your smash is not hit to his inside. If this flat smash is driven straight back at you, you can no longer smash. Your opponent, knowing you can only drive or drop, can move in closer to the net, secure in the knowledge that he can handle your drive much more easily than your smash. In this situation, you should not clear, otherwise you relinquish the offense. If your opponent anticipates a lot and moves all the way into the net, an occasional fast clear will keep him "honest" but this is not recommended as a standard procedure. A better shot, in this case, is either a half court drive or a quick drop hit crosscourt away from the incoming opponent. The ideal situation, of course, is not to allow yourself to get into this predicament—don't smash while off balance; instead, drop first and then you will be in position to get a good angle on the *next* clear.

Another technique used by experienced smashers is to smash with a change of pace. This can be achieved in two different ways, but each requires the same full arm movement used in the all out smash. Perhaps the better method for getting half to three quarter speed is to use the full arm movement but with little or no uncocking of the wrist. This is more likely to fool your opponent. Another way to cut down on the speed of the smash is to cut across the bird slightly, either by tilting the racket slightly sideways (which is difficult to hit to an exact spot because of the sideways tilt), or by tilting the racket backward and brushing the bird with the racket lengthwise in a downward stroke.

Figure 4

Regardless of which method you use, restrict its use. The slowed-down smash is far more effective when you have first "set-up" your opponent with full speed smashes. This tactic is far more effective against the type of defender who takes a full arm stroke, and who defends with both his forehand and backhand, and when this smash is hit to his inside wing (closest to the middle). (Fig. 4B) It can be effective also against a player who defends exclusively on his backhand but usually only if he is in his right alley (Fig. 4A). When he is on his left side of the court, this change of pace *can* work, particularly if he habitually attempts to return smashes to the smasher's backhand. The "slow ball" should be hit to his right hip.

Shorter players cannot get the same sharp, downward angle to their smashes as taller players and consequently have to use different tactics. Some make up for their lack of height by leaping high into the air as they smash. Some who are quick of foot, can make up for their basically poor smashing angle and seldom get caught out of position. A shorter player must do one of these things: either leap very high when smashing in order to get good angle, or use quick drops to move his opponent up, hoping to get a weak clear or to catch his opponent moving back and thus not set at his normal base for defending against the more flat smash. Even a taller player can use a flat smash to good effect if he directs it at a spot that cramps his opponent's arm movement. For instance, if your opponent prefers to meet your smashes on his backhand from a point somewhere between his waist and chest, as most defenders do, this means that he must be in closer to the net in order to hit the bird at that height (assuming that your smashes have been fairly well angled downward). Therefore the vulnerable spot for this type of defender is around shoulder or head height and slightly to your left of his right shoulder or head. (Fig. 3A and B, P. 28) Your smash must be hit outward and with maximum speed. He can effectively return, on his backhand, a well angled smash to his forehand side by bringing his backhand over to his forehand side, provided the bird is hit in an area from his waist to his chest. However, his arm movement becomes cramped and his return ineffective, if not missed outright, when the bird is hit at shoulder or head level on his forehand side. If he has returned your low smashes regularly and suddenly you hit to a spot higher and with speed, your chances of success are good. This flat smash at the right shoulder is an excellent means of coping with opponents who like to crowd the net and get to your drops quickly while they are still high, so they can push low, flat clears at you, hoping you will smash off balance and/or outward. Normally you should drop so as to get a high clear return which you can smash. However, if you use a drop every time under these circumstances, your opponents will soon realize this and will virtually walk to the net, no matter how much you make your drop look like a smash. To keep this from happening, you will be forced occasionally to use this flat smash at the right shoulder in order to keep them back. One caution about this cramping flat smash: if your opponent is tall and plays at a normal depth in his court, you run the risk of hitting the bird out beyond his baseline; better use the steeply angled downward smash against a tall player who plays back in the court.

When you have the bird up on your side, occasionally place a quick drop to a point slightly beyond the middle of the net from a point near either alley. The flight of this bird causes the opponent straight ahead of you to start to move for the drop, because the bird travels for most of its flight as though going to his half of the court but at the last second, he sees that it will land in his partner's half of the court. So both opponents let it drop, each thinking the other will hit it. The drop cannot be slow otherwise one of them will recover in time to get it back.

Evaluation Questions

Which is the safest return of the serve to use in men's doubles?

THE NETMAN'S ROLE

The smasher's partner up front plays a vital part in the effectiveness of any doubles play. He can be an asset or liability. His position in relation to the net is most important. He should be slightly to the left of the center line when the bird is up on his left, and in the middle of the court when his partner is smashing from his right. In both cases, his left foot should be advanced with his weight on the back foot; his racket should be up and his forearm and wrist cocked so he is able to hit a round-the-head shot or forehand. His depth in the court depends upon his height and quickness. Normally, he should be as far back as he can be and still cover the net in case the defender uses a drop shot as a reply to a smash. He should not be so far back that he interferes with his partner's follow-through, but far enough back to finish off a weak clear or drive. The members of most teams have an understanding regarding which shots the netman should take. In addition to the obvious weak returns, he usually takes either all crosscourt drives to both the backhand or forehand, or he attempts to cut off all accessible returns straight ahead. It is true that if the smasher always smashes to the inside of the opponent straight ahead of him, his partner at the net can expect most returns to be straight back and not crosscourt, making the netman more effective. However, if smashes always go to one area, this makes the opponents' job of defending much easier. Most smashers prefer to have their partner drop back slightly and protect against any crosscourt drive return, thereby giving the smasher more choice of spots at which to smash. In this case the opponents cannot anticipate so well, making the smasher much more effective.

The netman *must* keep his racket up with his forearm and wrist cocked in readiness for the return. There is usually no time to bring the racket back and forward in a full arm movement. Many an opportunity to

33

win a rally has been lost, or an error made, by netmen who waited until they could see where the bird was going before they brought the racket up. If his racket is not up and back, the netman should let the bird go past him rather than attempt to cut it off. His partner behind him has a better chance of keeping the bird in play than does he. A good rule for the netman to follow is to never attempt to cut off any drive return unless he has anticipated where it will be hit. There just is not enough time to look for a drive in more than one area and be consistently successful.

The netman must be careful not to form the habit of always hitting to one spot when he has a fairly weak but low return at the net which he can hit offensively but not a cripple that he can put on the floor. Many players tend to hit to the inside of the man straight ahead or to the middle, feeling that this is a safer target. *If you follow a pattern, it will be discovered by your opponents and used against you!* Use both alleys occasionally, especially the one to your left. Since most players defend on their backhand exclusively, this is a vulnerable spot.

One of the problems that arises in men's doubles is the netman's blocking of a shot that his partner behind him wants to make but cannot because of the netman's position at the net. For example, your partner has hit a smash more flat than he intended and the opponent straight ahead has leveled it off into a drive back at the smasher. Your opponent, realizing that your partner will not be able to smash again, moves in toward the net anticipating a drop. If your partner behind you tries to drop straight ahead, he must hit a perfect drop; since he is usually a little off balance and hurried by the return, his chances of hitting a near perfect drop are almost nil. His ideal return, under these circumstances, is a crosscourt drop or half court drive away from the netcrowding opponent straight ahead of him. However, if you, the netman, are back in your normal position in the middle of the court, you are blocking the path for your partner's intended shot. This problem arises more often in mixed doubles. (See Fig. 5, Page 60). You must work out with your partner where he wants you to go in such a circumstance—left, right, squat down, up or back. If you move over in front of the bird as it passes you, not only will you shield your partner's shot from the advancing opponent but you will also force your partner to hit to the correct spot. However, your move must be made instantly as the bird is coming back quite fast, leaving your teammate little time to see the opening.

An important shot that all netmen should develop, including the woman in mixed, is the *undercut dropshot.* The hairpin drop, described in Chapter 3, is very effective when both opponents are somewhat back from the net. But if an opponent is near the net, this drop must be perfectly executed or it will be put away by an opponent. Since seldom in men's doubles are *both* opponents back when net shots are made, you will need a shot that you can use when an opponent is fairly close to the net and when you do not want to give away the offense by clearing.

The undercut drop, should be met, ideally, when it is fairly close to net level. It is most easily executed as a return of a drop or net shot. The bird is hit with an undercutting or shoveling motion, with a slight downward or forward tilt of the racket. Depending upon how high the bird is met and how close it is to the net, the racket will follow-through across the net, especially if the bird is hit in the middle of the racket lengthwise. The motion should be sudden thus causing your opponent to move back, hesitate or at least blink. This undercutting action, if made straight forward with a *level* racket, *not* tilted sideways, will cause the bird to turn over as it crosses the net. This tumbling action makes any attempt to return it quite risky until the bird has straightened itself out. By that time, it will have fallen below the net.

RETURNS OF SERVE

There are two schools of thought regarding how to return an opponent's low serve. One says "put pressure on the server on every serve—rush every serve as much as possible—eventually the server will lose confidence and control." In some cases this is true, but not with most experienced players. Any mistakes by the rusher into the net or out of court give the opponents not only a point, but give the server more confidence. Simultaneously the rusher loses his confidence, or at least becomes more hesitant to continue this tactic.

The more conservative theory of return of serve advocates playing the return a little safer—"get them to lift and *then* attack." It is better to hit two or three safer shots and be sure of getting the attack than to gamble on one all out return. The author feels that this is the better system.

When receiving the serve in your right court, the left foot should be close to the front line and your racket up, ready to return the serve with your backhand. You should be alert for a drive serve to your backhand, since this serve can get to you the soonest. If a drive serve is attempted, drive it back downward with your backhand, preferably at the server or between him and the sideline. Then follow it on in to the net. From this position you will have time to change your grip and either move back for the flick or up and over for the low serve to the alley.

The body weight should be forward mostly on the left foot. If the serve is low, to either the center or to the alley, take a short step forward with the left foot, reach out and make whichever return you wish. This position allows you to move forward or backwards quickly. If your opponent flick serves, shove off the left foot and either leap into the air to intercept the flick, if this be possible, or take a long backward lunge off the left foot in a gliding or skipping motion. Your left foot should land behind the point where your right foot started. The quicker and farther back that you make this lunge, the better body position and balance you will have with which to make your smash.

35

Which shot is less risky when the bird is up to you, a smash or a drop?

Evaluation Questions

Players who like to rush every serve usually receive the serve in the right court with their forehand up, and take the drive serve with the round-the-head stroke. How the serve should be returned is a matter of preference and philosophy. Most players receive the serve in the left court with their forehands and follow the same procedures for the various serves as described in the right court.

Basically, there are only three returns of a low serve: 1) the drop, 2) the punch or drive at the server's partner in the back court and 3) the half court.

THE DROP RETURN. The *drop return* is usually made straight ahead and, *if executed well,* you get the offense right away. Most players do not wish to play a return drop with you standing right there, because it must be perfect, so instead the clear to your partner in back invariably results. A crosscourt drop return is not recommended as it must be perfect. Even if your opponent cannot "kill" it, he can contact it high since it travels toward him and away from you, and he can more safely re-drop, forcing you to clear and thereby lose the offense. To be effective, the drop must be executed with some quick or sudden movement of the arm and body. This causes the server to freeze momentarily; by the time he recovers, the bird is below the net on his side. If your drop is not perfect, he will move in immediately and put it away.

THE DRIVE RETURN. The *punch* or *drive return* at the server's partner in the back court is usually made to his backhand since that is usually his weaker "wing." However, to keep him "honest" vary your return to his forehand alley and at his right elbow if he defends primarily with his backhand. This will cramp his arm movement and usually produce either a winner or a weak return. One word of caution when aiming at his elbow:

if your opponent is tall and plays fairly deep in the court, the bird may go out over the baseline. Consider this possibility when you use this return. Also, you should check before your punch return, to see whether he has his forehand or backhand at the ready position. When a drive return is used, your partner should move up and you should step back a step after the return, with both of you playing sides. Both of you should be *as close to the net* as you can be and still handle a drive and, of course, a possible clear. Your opponent will not want to clear and give away the offense, and if he drives at either of you, he can be in trouble if either of you drive it back to the opposite side of the court from him. In effect, it is two against one if he drives. His most logical return is a drop with the hope of getting it below the net before either of you can contact it. Here is the crucial point which determines which side gains the offense: if you or your partner do not contact his drop close to or above net level, you have then lost the offense. So it is imperative that you both play in as close to the net as feasible. There may be times when perhaps your partner is not playing in as close as he should and is allowing the drop to get below the net, or you have guessed that your opponent is going to drop and you move in after you punch, anticipating the drop (Photo 2). You must make your move immediately so your partner knows whether your team is playing an up-

Photo 2

and-back or a sides formation. This is recommended as a surprise technique, not standard procedure, because it results in a rather neutral situation with both teams having a man up and one back. The sides formation gives you a two against one advantage, providing neither of you allow a successful drop to be made in front of you. This position, therefore, is more offensive and is favored by most teams.

Of course, the effectiveness of your opponent's serve will be a major factor in determining which side gains the offense. If the serve is mediocre, your return will be to your opponent's waist or knee. But even if it is an excellent low serve, if you are alert and meet the bird out in front of you as it crosses the net, you should be able to punch it so that it gets no higher than shoulder level of the back man.

THE HALF COURT RETURN. The ideal *half court* return of service should be hit so that it beats the netman and is dropping downward as it goes past him. The netman will usually start for the shot but seeing it behind him, will let it go for his partner in back. The back player, thinking that his partner at the net will take it, stops and the bird falls to the floor untouched. Even if the back man does get it, his return must be up, providing your team with the offense. The use of the half court shot is not restricted to the return of a serve. It is used during play occasionally in men's and women's doubles, but much more frequently in mixed doubles.

The half court return is used chiefly on the server's backhand alley since it is more difficult for the netman to get any power while reaching back on his backhand side. He can, however, reach back on his forehand and with wrist alone, either "kill" the bird or at least make an offensive shot. Chances of error are less on his forehand.

There are two positions that you can take after using a half court return of a serve: 1) Go on into the net and thus assume the attacking position while your partner smashes or drives when your opponents clear or drive and 2) The other is to drop back a step or two and play sides, as when you punch the return. The latter method is better if the server has anticipated and cuts off your half court. Being back a couple of steps, you at least have a chance to return his drive down the alley, whereas if you had gone on in, your partner would have had little or no chance to get it. You must make your move immediately one way or the other so your partner behind you can assume his responsibilities as either the back man in an up-and-back formation or as a member of a sides formation.

The half court return of a serve is the least used of the three basic returns because it is dangerous if not executed properly. Even when it is, if the server anticipates your half court by moving sideways and cutting it off, usually he can either win the rally outright or at least gain the offense. If you go in to the net after your half court, he can drive past you, usually for a winner. If you drop back a step or two after your half court return, he can drop in front of you. The main value of the half court return is that,

38

if used sparingly, it keeps the server back somewhat thus making your drop return of his serve more effective.

A fourth return of a serve, effective if used sparingly, is a variation of the half court return. Instead of the half court down the alley, it is hit a little to the *alley* side of the server and downward with medium pace. This is especially effective against a server who likes to anticipate half court shots down the alley. It gives him another possible return to think about and thus makes your half court and drop returns more effective. Usually he will be too late to recover; instead of continuing to the alley and out of the way so that his partner can hit it, he will try for it and miss. Many times, even if he continues sideways in order to let his partner take it, he blocks his partner's vision enough so that the bird falls untouched. The least that can happen is that the return has to be directed upward.

The three basic returns of serve can be broken down in terms of frequency of use as follows: The punch or drive return should be used approximately 80 per cent of the time (counting the variations of the spots at which to punch). The drop should be used 10-15 per cent of the time, and the half court 5-10 per cent. The drop and half court returns must be near perfect, otherwise your opponents will probably score a point outright. You can make a less than perfect drive return, however, and still keep the offense. Even if you should lose the offense, you still have a possible chance to win the rally.

ON DEFENSE

No matter how hard you try to keep the bird below the net on your opponents' side, sometimes you either will be forced to clear, or a clear would be the advisable shot. If both teams are equal in the ability of getting the bird up to their side, then the team with the better defense probably will be the winner.

There are two methods of returning a smash. One is strictly defensive—playing each smash back up high in the air, making sure that it is not intercepted by the netman and with the idea of attempting to wear out one or possibly both opponents. If one smasher does not have a well angled *or* hard smash, this technique might work if used persistently. However, some teams will switch off under these conditions, with the weaker or tiring smasher using a slower smash or drop to the alley straight ahead and following it in to the net to cover any drop that might be attempted. At the same time the former netman drops back and, because of the height of their clear, has ample time to take over the smashing. This is also a good technique to use when one member of the team is better at the net and wants to get there, yet is forced by his opponents to do most of the smashing.

On the whole in modern day badminton, however, both members of the better teams have good effective smashes and recognize that playing strictly defensively is a losing technique. Against a top smasher, there is no time to

39

start from a ready position with the racket directly in front of the body and still be able to return offensively either from the forehand or the backhand. By playing back deeper in the court a player *can* return from both wings but his clears then must be higher and almost completely defensive. Therefore, defending on the backhand exclusively is more prevalent since there is no backswing of the arm after the smash has been made—just one forward movement. This gives the defender an opportunity to counterattack. In this defense, both players move a little closer to the net in order to meet the bird higher. Your proximity to the net will depend on your reflexes and your opponent's smashing speed. Both players move over to approximately three feet inside of the extreme right line of their half of the court. (Fig. 3A-B, P. 28). From this position on the court, the arm can be brought over in front of, and to the right side of the body, while still using the backhand (Fig. 4A, P. 31). You cannot get as much forearm action with the backhand stroke while using it on your forehand side as you can on the normal backhand. However, if the wrist is used properly, power is not so important because you are using the speed of your opponent's smash in your stroke. Any shots beyond your reach on your right side will be out of court, or will be your partner's, depending upon which half of your court you are on. The body should be turned slightly toward the left sideline with the right foot forward. As the opponent smashes, the forearm and wrist must be cocked with the elbow bent and carried *high*, at, or slightly above, chest level. It is easier and quicker to lower the arm and racket for a low, well-angled smash than to raise both for a flat smash. It is particularly important to keep your arm and racket high when your opponent is about to smash from a point near his shoulder or head. This smash must be more flat and therefore higher. Knowing this can help you in anticipating at least the level of the flight of the bird. From this position the only action that is necessary is to uncock the forearm and wrist at the bird in one quick motion. This must be done in that split second in which you have determined its level of flight (shoulder, chest, waist, etc.) and its location.

One very important factor in executing this return is that you *must* contact the bird out in *front* of the body. Not only do you thus get the full uncocking effect of the forearm and wrist, but you also contact the bird at a *higher* point. The forearm should begin uncocking at almost the exact moment that your opponent contacts the bird. It should be in *motion* a fraction of a second *before* you have determined its exact destination. If you wait until you are sure and *then* uncock the forearm and wrist, you will probably be late. The closer to the net you can return his first smash, the lower you will be able to return his second and each succeeding smash; finally you will have leveled off his smash into a net-level drive. Sometimes this can be done on his first smash, if he doesn't get good downward angle. Here then is another reason for always getting *to* the bird as soon as possible, whether it be a smash or a drop: If you can force him to smash from around shoulder or head height, his smash *must* be more flat, giving you the opportunity to level it out into a drive back at him or to drive cross-court past his netman.

When you have returned a smash to your opponent's shoulder or head, both you and your partner must be particularly alert for a drop because that is what he *should* do in order to get a high clear from you which he can then properly angle downward. This is where many teams allow an opponent to "get off the hook." The sooner you can get to his drop, the more you and your partner can push him around until you are presented with a weak shot or a clear.

As long as either or both of your opponents continue to smash to the same spot (e.g., to the midcourt side of the player straight ahead of the smasher), then your job of defending becomes simplified considerably. If the opposing netman is looking for your return straight ahead, then you can crosscourt without too much fear of having it cut off. If he is protecting the crosscourt area for his partner, then the straight ahead return is your best reply. Each return is much easier to control and can be hit more offensively if you know where the smasher is directing his smashes. If he varies his attack, your return should be straight ahead, since most smashers who hit to all areas want their partners to protect for them against crosscourt return.

Sometimes you must temporarily defend the whole court (your partner has fallen or dropped his racket). A good maneuver that works occasionally is to fake a move toward your partner, as if to cover a smash near him, thus leaving an apparent opening. As your opponent is about to contact the bird, move back but anticipate the smash at the "opening." More often than not, that is where the bird will be.

COMMON DOUBLES SITUATIONS

Having gained the offense, it is a *better policy* to smash than to drop. There is less chance for error in a smash than in a drop. Exceptions to this rule are if you are off balance, are tiring, or if your opponents are hanging back in the court to better return your smashes.

There are rallies in doubles play when neither side really has the offense, at least momentarily. The most common example of this is when the receiver stays at the net after punching the return of the serve at the back man. The server's partner cannot safely drop with an opponent up at the net, so his logical move is a drive or half court past the netman. Thus a neutral situation arises with each side having a man up and one back. If the netman on both teams remains up, then it becomes a battle between the two back men to determine which can out-drive the other or force a weak return which his partner at the net can put away.

Frequently, however, the netman will step back a couple of steps anticipating a crosscourt drive, especially when he feels his teammate has been out-maneuvered. The threat that the opposing netman will step back

When you have levelled out your opponent's smash to his shoulder, what shot should you expect from him?

Evaluation Questions

and intercept poses probably the most difficult situation that any player has to cope with in doubles. If you drive crosscourt, the opposing netman can intercept and usually win the point outright. If you drop, and the opposing netman has not stepped back too far, as is usually the case, you must drop perfectly or he will re-drop or put it away. The pace of the drive or flat smash is so fast that it is virtually impossible to watch the bird and the opposing netman at the same time. Therefore, if your opponents when each is the netman, habitually move back in this situation, the best thing for you, the back player, to do is either to drive straight back to the inside of the opposing back man (so as to cramp his arm movement on his next shot), or to half court straight back down the alley away from your opponents' netman.

Both the above half court and drive should be hit with a body fake. The body goes sideways in the direction that the crosscourt drive should go, luring the opposing netman in that direction which is away from the intended spot. The half court should be guided so it is dropping after it crosses the net, hopefully quite low before it is returned from a spot in the alley, halfway back. The third and least desirable alternative is a drop straight ahead. This is risky and requires a lot of "touch." Regardless of which shot is used, your partner at the net has one of two moves: 1) He can move back and you come up (sides formation) forcing their back man to drop. With both of you fairly close to the net, your opponent must execute a near perfect drop, for otherwise you either have a weak shot to put away, or you can drop it and thus gain the offensive. 2) The other alternative is for your netman to stay in and guard against a close drop. In this case the opposing back man is given a choice of four areas to which to hit his shot: a half court to either side, or a drive to either side. The number one alternative is recommended as you give your opponent less choice of shots. The net-

Evaluation Questions

Which is the safest return of the serve in mixed doubles?

man *must* make his move instantly however for otherwise his partner may become confused.

A word of advice is in order here. In the above and similar situations where your opponent has hit a drop or a serve that is a few inches higher than it should be, the inexperienced, eager player quite often will attempt to "kill" it. It is much better to rush in *as if* to "kill" but instead, to drop it even though you then take two or three smashes to win the point. This action will make your punch or drive much more effective when you do have a reasonably sure "kill." Missing what seems to be an easy "kill" can be very upsetting and the ensuing loss of confidence can cause you to miss real setups later on. So when in doubt, particularly at the beginning of a match when you tend to be a little nervous or toward the end when you might be tiring, it is better to fake a "kill" but drop instead. Of course, circumstances vary from match to match. If your opponents have been handling your partner's smashes quite easily and consistently, perhaps the "kill" attempt would be better.

SPECIAL DOUBLES SITUATIONS

1. When your partner is serving to the left court, you should be a little to the left of and behind your partner and in the middle when he serves to the right court. Your exact position sideways will vary slightly depending upon whether your partner serves to the middle or to the alley. Be sure to maintain visibility of the bird at all times—as your partner follows his serve to the net, he can block your vision at the precise moment that your opponent returns the serve.

Your depth in the court will depend on the effectiveness of your partner's serve and how your opponents have been returning it. If one or both

43

opponents use one type of return exclusively, you can adjust your position up or back accordingly.

2. One of the most common mistakes is to attempt to hit the flick serve to within inches of the receiver's backhand and then miss. If you fool him, it doesn't matter whether the flick goes to his forehand or backhand. At least get the bird in play and give him a chance to miss it!

3. Talk to your partner during play when there is any question as to who should hit a shot. Many a bird has dropped to the floor because each thought the other was going to hit it. It should be noted though that the rules specify that any talking or yelling must take place *after* the bird has been hit by your opponents and while it is on *your* side of the net (distraction rule).

4. When smashing a *high* clear, you will have time to take a quick look to see with which wing your opponent straight ahead will be defending. This information can be of value in preventing awkward returns. When you play against a defender who deliberately sets his defense one way as you look and then changes as you hit, it becomes a guessing game with you holding the advantage *if* you *angle* your smash downward severely. Do not try this procedure on the low flick or punch clears as there is not enough time and you will make too many errors trying to see how he defends.

5. When one of your opponents is less effective in returning smashes, concentrate your smashes at him. This is no problem when he is straight ahead of you but when he is crosscourt, you run the risk of his being able to place your crosscourt smash to the other side of the court, thereby forcing you to scramble. Therefore the best procedure is to drop to *his* side of the *middle* so that the follow-through of his arm action will tend to place his clear straight ahead of him. When you move over a few steps you then have the bird and your weaker opponent exactly where you want them; you will therefore, be able to smash more safely.

6. There is one situation in smashing that must be resolved if your teamwork is to be effective. This is when a return of your team's smash is fairly weak, but is back far enough so that if your netman is to take it he has to reach behind him as he is moving backwards. The netman is usually afraid of colliding with his teammate and so does not get as far back and as far behind the bird as he should. Obviously then he cannot be as powerful or hit as well-angled a smash as could his teammate behind him. The netman, therefore, should not attempt to hit this kind of shot but should immediately yell "yours" and move over and slightly backward toward the half of the court away from the bird. This will give the back man a full uninhibited swing and a better chance to put the bird away. For an instant, both players are then side by side, *both* ready to smash again, if necessary.

7. One of the most difficult teams to play is one which includes a left handed opponent. During a match there will be at least four or five rallies won by this combination that would not have been won were both right

Evaluation Questions

Which partner should not, as a rule, crosscourt a punch return of the serve?

handed. There *should* be no great problem if at the beginning of each rally you simply note which one is up and which one is back, before the serve. It is after the rally has been in progress for a few exchanges that it is easy to lose track of "who is where" on the court. You must stay constantly alert—take advantage of any time that you may get to note the position of each player (such as during high clears).

8. A problem in teamwork that arises quite frequently in men's and women's doubles, but more frequently in mixed doubles, concerns your team's handling of a half court return. The *absolute* fixing of responsibility for this shot is not advisable. The netman definitely takes all drops and the back man takes all drives and clears. But the half court ideally should go to a spot halfway between the netman and the back man. Therefore, *unless* the netman has anticipated a half court by moving sidewards *only*, he should let the back man take it. Usually the bird is past the netman before he can determine that it is a half court anyway. His partner can do much more with the bird, even though it may be a little lower when he contacts it, because he can contact it out in front of himself.

Sometimes the netman will start sideways, anticipating a half court, but, realizing that he will not be able to make an effective shot, he stops. His back partner should *not* be faked out by this movement. He should not stop going for the bird until he sees his netman actually hit it. He still has ample time to cover the back part of his court regardless of what shot is made. If the back man drives or clears, the netman merely moves back and sideward a step or two to cover half the court opposite from the original half court, thus putting both players into a sides position to attack (if a drive is made) or to defend (if a clear).

9. Under *most* situations in doubles play, the netman should always keep his eyes on the bird, even when it is behind him, particularly if his

45

When either the man or the woman serves in mixed doubles, can you halfcourt return ten out of ten good low serves that the opponent must contact below the waist? below the knees?

Evaluation Questions

partner uses overhead drops quite frequently rather than smashes. The net-man's distance from the net will vary in accordance with what his partner does with the bird. When his partner smashes, he should be farther back, to protect against crosscourt return drives or to be behind the bird for a "kill." When a drop is made, he should move in close to the net to discourage the opponents from re-dropping. If you, the netman, look back as your partner contacts the bird, you can get a jump on the bird *when* he drops, enabling you to get to the net before your opponent contacts your partner's drop.

If for the purpose of surprise, your partner uses an attacking clear to keep an opponent back who likes to crowd the net, you have more time to move back in a defensive position if you were watching when the clear was hit.

When you are the netman in a more or less neutral situation (both teams having a man up and a man back), the same principle applies. The sooner you know what shot your partner is making, the sooner you can go to the proper spot to cover your opponents' reply to your partner's shot.

One word of caution. If you wear glasses, wear *plastic lenses*. You cannot be sure that your partner will always be accurate or will hit to the expected place.

10. Sometimes you can win a quick point by deliberately looking away from your intended target, (e.g., when serving from the right court, look at the alley but serve a drive to his backhand).

11. Whenever possible, help your partner judge whether birds are in or out. Birds hit at a very fast pace, for example a flat smash, are difficult to judge. On clears and crosscourt drops or drives, however, you can help considerably. Your partner's attention must be on the bird but you can watch both the bird and its relationship to the line. In particular you should

be ready to shout "out" or "no," when he is receiving a flick or drive serve. If you position yourself along the middle line just where it intersects the back service line, you can warn him of drive serves that are wide (this is the serve that will get to him the soonest). Secondly, if they flick, you are also in position to judge whether or not it is long. It should be understood that you will speak only when it is out so that he can react quickly and without confusion.

12. A word on setting when your team has reached 13 or 14 first. At 14 all, it is wiser to choose three. At 13 all, much will depend on whether one or none are down, whether their better server is down or not, who won the first game, if the game in question is the second, and how well your team has been serving and returning the serve.

13. A variation of doubles which can speed up your reflexes and footwork is to play with three players on a side (Tribles). The Thailand Thomas Cup Team uses this device to improve the quickness of eye and foot of its doubles players. A complete new set of playing procedures and formations must be established for this game (i.e., where all three go on offense, defense, serve, return of serve as well as how many serves to a side, etc.). This game has not been used extensively in this country but its possibilities are great, at least for three shorter players. Should you and your partner not find sufficient competition among the local duos, you can get good opposition from a Tribles team.

WOMEN'S DOUBLES

For the most part, the basic fundamentals are the same for women's and men's doubles (i.e., to keep the bird going down, same defensive and offensive positions, etc.). The main difference is that in women's doubles the clear, the drop, and the flick serve are used much more frequently. This is because most women's smashes are not as strong (thereby making the return of smashes a much more effective weapon), and because most women are not quite as quick in covering the court. There must, therefore, be more finesse and out-maneuvering of one or both opponents *before* the smash, much the same as in singles.

Knowing that no one will hesitate to use the flick serve and that the resultant smash will be returned fairly consistently, one is less likely to rush the serve. This situation makes the low serve more effective. Of course, if both women partners have a powerful smash, then by all means it should be used for the smash is the safest shot to employ from overhead, provided the smasher is on balance and *if* she meets the bird in front of her so she can angle it downward sharply.

4

Mixed Doubles

Mixed doubles is a *far* more complex game than it appears to the casual observer. There is a much greater variety of situations and patterns of play than in either men's or women's doubles. One shot may be the best to use at a particular point in a rally but on the very next exchange it may be the worst.

FORMATIONS USED

Basically, the shots used in mixed play are the same as in men's doubles. The main differences stem from the formation used. In the usual mixed match, both women play up close to the net, and the men are responsible for all shots to the backcourt area. This is because women are not fast or strong enough to compete with a top male from the back court. While there have been champion mixed teams where the woman was strong enough to play a modification of the men's doubles formation, this system is used only under certain specific circumstances (such as during the man's return of serve, when the bird has to be lifted, or when the man has been out-maneuvered).

During conventional mixed play, where opposing men play in the back court and the women protect the net area, it is even more important to keep the bird *going down* than it is in men's doubles. In men's doubles, it is possible to clear and still win a fair percentage of rallies. This is because both men drop back side by side and so can cover the whole court. However, whether the woman stays in at the net or drops back to help defend, the odds favor the smashing team. If she stays up, the smasher can hit to either alley. If she drops back to a temporary sides position, her team isn't going to win a high percent of these rallies. The best formation is women up, men back, and never lift the bird.

DETERMINING THE STYLE TO BE USED. The style and patterns of play in mixed doubles must be largely dictated by the abilities and style of the man. If a team is to be fully effective, the woman must realize this and adapt *her* play in order to exploit his strong points. But the man must be able to play so that his partner can *generally* expect him to hit the shot which is correct for a particular situation. If either repeatedly plays the same shot in a specific situation, the opponents will easily anticipate the play. In this game, either partner can make the other look good or poor, depending upon how shots are executed and upon their choice.

If the man is better than the opposing man at the driving game, it makes sense to play this type of game. If he is better at the slower game, relying on touch to get the bird down with half courts and occasionally drops, then this is how the team should play. Because both styles almost completely exclude the woman until a weak return is forced, many women resent this; getting impatient to get into the play, they often drop back and attempt to hit a drive or a half court that would better have been left to the man. The woman in mixed doubles play must face the fact that the majority of shots during play are, or at least should be, hit by the man. She must, therefore, be patient but *always ready* to hit the shot that she should. The woman's part of the play is subtle; it can be very satisfying and highly effective.

THE SERVE

Since the man is usually responsible for the backcourt area, he serves from a point farther back than he does in men's doubles. The exact distance from the net will vary in accordance with his ability to cover any return of his serve effectively. Normally it will be about the same depth as that used when his partner is serving. The woman serves from the usual men's and women's doubles position near the front service line.

Most all serves should be low but varied with an occasional flick to keep the rushing type of receiver "honest." If the opposing woman is a little weak from her overhead position, you might exploit this weakness by serving more flicks, or perhaps a high singles type of serve will be effective. *On any serve,* the left foot should be forward. When serving to the left court, the left foot is brought sidewards to the left as the bird is hit to form a semi-crouch and a sound base from which to move instantly to any return of your serve. When serving to the right court, the right foot is similarly brought to the right.

During the man's serve, the woman is up at the net, just how close depends on her quickness and ability to meet any drop before it gets below the net. Some teams place the woman on the left side of the net on all serves delivered by the man, whether to the left or right court. This is done to encourage half courts to the woman's forehand which she can return more effectively than those from her backhand. Crosscourt drop returns

At what height does it become dangerous to contact the bird for a drive, A, B, C, D?

Evaluation Questions

THE DRIVE

are discouraged when the man serves to the alley from his left court. However, if the serve is good and low it really doesn't make any difference on which side she stands.

Many teams serve to the alley to combat rushing tactics but this opens up the court for more return angles. However, in mixed, this restricts the man's punch return to the straight ahead area. If he crosses his punch return from his alley, he is out of position for the next drive straight ahead, which usually is a winner.

THE RETURN OF SERVE. This is the part of mixed doubles that is the most complex and difficult to master and can be disasterous if not executed sensibly and with variety. There are so many possible returns, some better than others, that it can be very complicated. It is not unusual to see a team run a string of six or eight points on one person's serve, usually the woman's. This is due partly to the excellence of the woman's serve, and partly to the opponents' improper choice of return or lack of variety of returns. When both opponents attempt to make their returns too good, the resulting errors add still more points for the serving side.

The same returns of service are used in mixed as in men's and women's doubles (drop, half court, and punch drive). However, there are situations in mixed where it is advisable *not* to use the drop or punch drive as your return. The half court is hit more often to the woman's backhand alley. Even though the half court is the safest over-all return, there are times when either a drop or a punch return would be better. There are also conditions where a certain return is all right for the woman, but a little too risky for the man to use under the same circumstances.

THE DROP RETURN OF SERVICE. The drop should mainly be used as a reply when the opposing woman is serving. Place it in the alley farthest

Diagram: D
THE DRIVE

from her. Of course, any fake (see Chapter 4 on Drop Return of Serve) to hold her back momentarily will make your drop more effective. The drop is a better return for the *woman* than the man because since she stays in, she can concentrate on moving to the bird and making a good close drop. The man must be conscious of protecting the backcourt, so consequently his drop *must* be very close to the net—otherwise he must be prepared to see the bird punched behind him. Even if the woman hits a mediocre drop, her partner has a good chance to handle any punch drive that the opposing woman might try, because he is on balance and set for it.

It is best for *neither* of you to use a drop as a return of the man's serve except as a shot to keep their net player from laying back for your half court returns. The opposing woman is closer to the net than when she is serving and in this situation she does not have the added burden of concentrating on her serve. The one exception to this rule is when the man serves to the alley of the first court. In order for him to have access to the alley, his partner must be positioned a little back and over in the alley. This leaves their right front area open for a quick, sliced crosscourt drop. Of course, if the man serves to the alley of your left court and his partner is playing straight ahead of you, a backhand crosscourt drop could be used.

THE HALF COURT RETURN OF SERVE. This is the safest and most used of the three returns. Its execution has been covered in Chapter 4. It must be hit a little deeper into the opponents' court when sent to the *forehand* alley of the woman because she can reach back and still make an effective shot from this side with her wrist only. As in the drop return, the woman can make a less than perfect half court return of serve, and since the man is back, your team can still recover and get out of trouble. If the *man* hits a less than perfect half court, however, you can be in trouble depending upon to which alley the shot was sent—if to her forehand, you will usually

How can you avoid being faked out of position?

Evaluation Questions

lose that rally and, worse yet, a point. You still have a reasonable chance to recover and win the rally if the half court was sent to her backhand, depending, of course, on how effective her backhand is.

The man *must* mix up his half court and drop returns when the opposing woman is serving in order to keep her from anticipating his shot; the more stereotyped the return, the greater the risk of losing *points*. Since they only lose a serve, they can afford to take chances. Since *you can lose points when they serve*, you should not take unnecessary chances or allow your opponents the luxury of a high percentage guess, as when you overdo either of the two riskier returns. Even though the half court is the safest of the three returns, it too is risky if overused. If the opposing woman knows that you, the man, half court three out of four times, practically all she has to do is walk over sideways to the alley and drive it past you for a point.

When the opposing man is serving, the half court is a good variant to the punch drive, but it should not be overdone here either because the woman is better prepared to handle it than when she is serving.

THE PUNCH OR DRIVE RETURN OF SERVE. The punch ranks along with the half court as a safe return of the serve *if* used properly. The *woman* can crosscourt her punch without serious consequences as long as she keeps it low. Her partner is in position behind her to cover a drive to either back corner. The man should normally restrict its use to straight ahead, *especially* if the serve is to his alley. If either opponent serves to the *middle*, then you can risk a crosscourt punch to keep him honest or to hit to his weaker side. You will have time to get back and cover his counter-drive if you punch from the middle.

The punch return is more effective for both members of your team when it is used against the opposing man's serve. When the woman opponent serves to the middle, either of you can punch fairly safely to either side. When she serves to the alley, your woman is better off if she uses a punch back at the man and not to the corners. This cuts down his angle of possible return and she is less likely to be caught by a quick drop away from her.

Basically, you both should alternately use the drop and the halfcourt to keep the opposing woman guessing, and the half court and the punch drive to keep the opposing man off balance or cramped in his stroking. Neither of you can make an *effective* return of *any* serve if you allow the bird to get too low. Any attempt to fool your opponent which involves allowing the bird to drop only gives your opponent time to recover and gives away the offense. When either of you are being served to, you must be as close to the front line as you can and still be able to cover a flick or a drive. You must be crouched and coiled to get to the bird as soon as possible with your arm reaching out in front of you to meet it. Then, and *only* then, do you have an equal chance to win the rally against a *good* server.

CONVENTIONAL PLAY PATTERNS

Since it is practically suicidal to clear in conventional mixed doubles, the half court and drive shots are far more prevalent than in men's doubles.

THE DRIVE

To gain a weak return, the drive by the man, and the punch drive by the woman should be used *anytime* the opposing man is out of position with but one exception: when the opposing woman, knowing her partner is out of position, steps back to intercept your crosscourt drive, a better shot is a drop either straight ahead or crosscourt. If his previous shot was a half court, you will have time to see her move back. If the previous shot was a drive, this poses one of the most difficult situations for the man in all of mixed doubles play. You will not have time in this case to look at her and to drive also. You will just have to guess in accordance with what she usually does—but *above all*, your drop must look as though you are going to drive, i.e., sliced and with a full arm motion. If you do decide to drive, the tendency is to play your crosscourt a little safer because you know the man will not get your shot. But *don't* take anything off your drive, either in speed or height above the net, if she *has* been stepping back, for you will give her an easier shot to handle if you do.

Other uses of the drive depend on two additional factors: 1) The relative ability of both men to cover the court from sideline to sideline, and 2) How high you are able to contact the bird. Obviously if you are better at driving and covering the court when your opponent drives, it would be to your advantage for you and your partner to drive until you get a weak shot which one of you can "kill" at the net. In this situation, where you have the edge, the woman should play a little farther back and to the alley closest to the bird; she should *not* intercept drives, but should be in position to put away a half court should your opponent try that in

53

When playing conventional mixed doubles is A or B a better return of the opponent's drop?

Evaluation Questions

RETURNING A DROP

his effort to slow the pace to his advantage. He will have more difficulty in hitting a drop from your drive than he will a half court shot. His drop *must* be quite finely executed or your partner has a "kill." His halfcourt can be less than perfect and still not get him into too much trouble *if* your woman partner is playing in the normal position nearer the net. If she is back a little she can make an offensive shot, if not win the rally outright. Of course, if the situation is reversed, and the opposing man has you out of position, a verbal signal is necessary to alert your partner to step back and attempt to intercept any crosscourt drives, *nothing else.* Usually you will have time to get to any shot which is high enough to get *over* her racket.

The *most important* consideration when driving is how high the bird is contacted. If you hit it at waist level or above, you can make an offensive shot, which is the purpose of the drive. The lower the bird is contacted below your waist, the less offensive can be your next shot. Unless you have the opposing man completely out of position on one side of the court, any drive initiated at knee level or below will probably get you into trouble.

The next most important factor in driving is the intended destination of the bird. *Normally* most drives are hit straight ahead down the alley, until either you feel that you have the advantage (i.e., the bird is high enough for you to try for a crosscourt winner) or until you want to use the crosscourt as a surprise shot to keep your opponent from "laying" for the straight ahead.

You must always attempt to *play your strengths* as well as *play to your opponent's weakness.* If you and your opponent have equal forehands but your backhand is superior to his, you should not be afraid to crosscourt a drive anytime from your backhand.

If you overplay your drives to his backhand, however, he can better prepare a variety of shots from that side. So it will be necessary to draw

Diagram: E

RETURNING A DROP

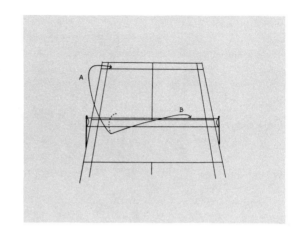

your opponent to his forehand side from time to time before hitting your crosscourt backhand. An excellent procedure for opening up his backhand is to use a half court shot to his forehand. Assuming that it is a good one which he must hit from around his knees, he won't drop because a drop must be perfect, with your partner right there at the net. He won't want to drive either crosscourt or straight ahead because these shots will come back and down very quickly and catch him out of position. About the only reasonable return that is open to him is a half court to your backhand. If your net player stays in position at the net and so is in no danger from your swing or follow through, you can slap it crosscourt, usually for an outright winner. Partners should have a mutual understanding of exactly what each will do in situations like this so opportunities are not lost.

There is one situation in which the man must *not* drive straight ahead to the *alley.* This is when your opponent has placed the bird just far enough away from you on a drive down an alley so that you cannot use a cocked forearm, thereby making your return drive ineffective. The natural tendency is to hit the drive down the alley. Because such a drive would be fairly weak, your opponent can easily slap it back crosscourt before you can even recover your balance. There are two alternatives when in this plight. Slow the pace down in order to gain time to recover your balance by hitting a straight-ahead drop or half court. If you must use a drive because the opposing woman has been pouncing on your half courts and drops, your drive should be pulled, with your wrist, to the inside of the man. He then will not be able to crosscourt effectively and you will still be in the rally.

A very similar situation arises for the woman when running toward a sideline to return an opponent's half court. If she is barely able to reach it, she should *not* attempt to drive it hard straight ahead down the alley where the opposing man is expecting it. He can crosscourt drop his return for a

55

winner before she can recover her balance. As in her partner's case, she should pull it with her wrist to the inside of the man if she decides to drive or she should half court it downwards. If there is an opening so a drop could be used, this would be a better shot.

Most women do not ever look back in mixed to see what shot is being played because drives are to be expected in this game. Also since there have been accidents which caused the loss of sight by doing so, it is not advisable to take this chance. When you have a few years' experience, you will learn that under certain situations you can safely take a quick look in order to give yourself that fraction of a second jump that may spell the difference between an offensive or a defensive shot. In the meantime, don't take chances.

Both of you should be prepared for your opponents to return the bird in whatever manner will take the least time to get to you, therefore expect the straight ahead drive first. A crosscourt return of any variety takes longer to get to its destination (the woman at the net therefore should look for a half court straight ahead before a crosscourt half court). Of course, if your opponent always crosses his or her shots, you simply reverse the rule as you play that particular person. A top player will not always do the same thing every time; if he did, he would not be tops.

THE HALF COURT DURING PLAY

The half court is a safer shot to use in mixed than in men's doubles because the woman is not usually as quick, nor does she have the reach that a man would have under the same circumstances in men's doubles. The half court is *usually* placed to the backhand alley of the woman, either to force a higher return so that one of you can then hit a more offensive shot, or to get yourself out of trouble when you have been forced to contact the bird from a lower point than you would have liked. Regardless of the reason, a body fake away from its intended mark, will often make your opponents move momentarily in the direction away from where you want the half court to go. Some women have been fooled so many times on this fake that it becomes an automatic signal to go opposite of the fake and to put the bird away. This being the case, if you can crossdrop in the direction of your body fake, you can keep her "honest"; otherwise don't use a fake.

A third, less frequent use for the half court, but a good one, occurs when the man has been caught slightly out of position, sideways, and you must slow down the pace of your opponent's drive in order to be on balance and in position for his next return as discussed earlier.

The half court to the woman's backhand should not be used exclusively or she will "lay" for it. When she is straight ahead of you, the sliced crosscourt half court with a full arm motion to either alley can be invaluable in getting the bird up to your side.

56

DEFENDING AGAINST THE SMASH

As much as you try never to hit the bird up in mixed doubles, there *will* be times when it will be necessary to do so. The flick serve, against a particularly effective rusher, is one example. How do you defend under these circumstances? There are two accepted methods. One method utilizes the ability of the woman to return smashes. In this case she drops all the way back for the first smash, defending half of the court, as in men's and women's doubles, and she remains there until either she or her partner is able to level off a smash to the point that it would be dangerous for the opposing man to smash again. At this point, the woman moves in again to the net ready to pounce on any loose drop shots.

In the second method, the woman steps back only one or two steps at the most, with her racket back on the alley side farthest from the man. She *must* *have* her racket moving *forward, as* they smash, in anticipation of a smash to that *one alley only.* The man has a better chance to return smashes from any *other* part of the court. If the woman stayed up at the net and did not attempt to return the smash, his only chance is to guess to which alley they will smash. This second method is a requirement when either partner *flick* serves as, in this event, the woman will not have time to move back to defend half of the court. This method assumes that the woman, being closer to the net, will be responsible for drops to her half of the court, as soon as she sees that the smash is not coming to her alley.

When using the high serve or when forced to hit a high defensive clear to your opponents' baseline, either method can be used. The effectiveness of your opponents' smashes and your woman partner's return of smashes will determine which method is the best for you. Perhaps it will be one method when the man smashes and the other when the opposing woman is smashing. In response to a high serve or clear, the woman should move sideways to a point crosscourt to the smasher, if she is not already there. The crosscourt takes longer to get to its destination and, if returned, can either get the hitter into serious trouble or win the rally outright for your team. She will *not* have time to go crosscourt on a flick serve by the man.

The standard reply by either of you to a flick serve is the smash. You must of course be careful not to overdo the smash to any one spot or you will be in trouble. Any mistake and you lose a point. The only exception is when both opponents are playing straight sides as in men's doubles. In this case, the drop should be used occasionally, especially when you are slightly off balance.

PROBLEM SITUATIONS DURING PLAY

1. A very common problem in mixed doubles teamwork arises when the woman has been caught out of position and the man must come to the net to cover a drop. His usual reply will be to re-drop. He cannot stay there, however, for an opponent's return drop because the whole backcourt

is open. Consequently the woman *must* go to the area of his drop immediately, thus releasing the man to cover the back area. Many women in this situation forget they are playing mixed doubles and start to move back as they would and should when playing women's doubles. To move back is a natural reaction but the man *can* cover the backcourt if he knows that his partner will take the next drop.

2. There are times during play and occasionally on the punch return of serve, when one of you will hit a shot—usually a drive to the man or a halfcourt to the woman—that "beats" the opponents (i.e., they must contact the bird from some point behind them). When this happens, most players cannot crosscourt the next shot, especially one from their backhand. *Both* of you then should move over in front of the bird, the woman moving up in anticipation of a drop and the man ready for a drive or half court. The woman should not allow some fake to keep her back, thus allowing the opponents to drop, thereby getting the bird down below the net. When a woman hangs back, this is probably because she does this in women's doubles as part of her teamwork. But she *must constantly remember* that when she is playing mixed doubles that her responsibilities are different.

3. Another fairly common instance when the woman forgets that she has a partner behind her occurs when the opposing man comes in to hit a defensive shot (from below his knees). He "holds" his shot as if to flick. (This is a very common technique but usually works only on the uninitiated). So the woman, forgetting she is not playing women's doubles, "sees through" the fake and instinctively starts back, only to have the opposing man block a drop shot in front of her. Thus an offensive situation has been turned into a defensive one.

4. The woman must *never* allow the opposing man to intimidate her by any movement or fake when he has to contact the bird from *below* the level of the net. It is understandable to want to duck if he gets a set-up to hit. But he can't hurt her, either physically or strategically when he has to hit the bird somewhat *upwards*. The secret of not being out-faked is to *watch the face of the racket as it is about to meet the bird*. Do *not* watch anything else—not body fakes or sweeping arm movements, just the racket. Remember, the bird can go in only *one* direction. If the face of the racket is moving to your left, the bird *must* go in that direction regardless of what the hitter's body may be doing. If you watch the *racket* and wait for the bird to be hit before you move, you will never be fooled.

5. Some teams get quite perturbed when the woman has a comparatively weak smash and the opponents take advantage of this by serving high to her consistently. There is no need for this if certain basic procedures are followed. Your team will not be hurt by your opponents' use of either the flick or the deliberate high serve if the woman will get *behind* the serve so that she can be moving toward her base at the net after her smash. There is no excuse for not doing this when the opponents serve high. When they flick serve, however, the woman might not be able to get her body behind

the bird and so may have to hit it while going backward. Assuming that she can smash and still recover soon enough to get to the net for a drop return, she should smash to the inside of the man straight ahead, so as to make a crosscourt drop by him more difficult. But should she be caught off balance and unable to get to the net to cover a drop, it would be better to encourage the opposing man to crosscourt drop his return to her partner's side; he can more easily play the drop and at the same time not get in his partner's way as she comes in toward the net.

The woman should make every effort to *angle the smash downward*. The speed of the smash is not as important, in this instance, as is the angle. In fact, speed can work against your team. The faster the smash, the faster the bird will come back when returned.

If the opponents serve a flick, the man may have to cover a drop return of the woman's smash. However, this should only occur when the woman can't get up to the net and still meet the bird fairly high. She should *always*, however, be able to get to a drop on her half of the net after her smash of the high, singles type serve. The man must be able to rely on the fact that the woman will not hang back after her smash so that he can cover both the first drop, if he has to, and a clear.

6. There is one situation involving half court shots which women often allow to go on for far too many exchanges. This occurs when one man hits a half court to the opponent's backhand alley which the opposing man is afraid to either drop or drive because he has to contact it too low. If he is going to hit a return half court that is not too high, he must fake with his body and arm as if to drive. In many instances this kind of cat-and-mouse play between the men will go on for three or four exchanges, each woman being faked out by the opposing man. Perhaps the woman on the backhand side might have a good reason for not attempting a backhand smash or drive, but certainly the woman on the forehand side should put away at least the second half court to her forehand alley; this she can do if she watches the racket only and steps sideward to the alley.

7. In the above situation, the woman should realize that the opposing woman's position on the court almost always blocks her partner's path for a crosscourt drop. Even if he wanted to, he would run too great a risk of hitting his own partner if, in this situation, he tried to crosscourt a drop or half court. This knowledge *should* free the woman to anticipate the half court straight ahead. (See Fig. 5)

When the situation is reversed and your partner is blocking your path so you cannot crosscourt drop, you should mutually understand that the moment she sees that the opposing man has hit a half court which she cannot safely hit that she will move *up* almost to the net, but not *over* in front of the bird. This will give her partner the option of sending a crosscourt drop or half court, as well as a straight ahead half court.

8. Every man has had numerous occasions in mixed play when he could have taken one step up and slapped an opponent's half court shot for

Figure 5

a crosscourt winner, but could not because his partner had moved back. Reaching behind her, all she can do is weakly return what should have been a winner. One *basic* rule for women in mixed doubles, as well as for the netman in men's, is: *when in doubt, let it go.* The partner in back has more time, better position, and the body balance to do more with the bird. A concommitant rule: if the woman has already started to move backward, she should instantly move back up to the net, well out of the way of her partner's swing and follow-through. Otherwise his return will have to be limited to a less severe stroke, for fear of hitting her. A good policy to follow under these circumstances is for the woman *never* to go for a crosscourt or straight ahead half court unless she has anticipated it by moving *sidewards* only. Her partner has a better chance to drive for a winner because the opposing man is out of position as a result of the fact that he is near the alley where he initiated the half court.

This problem more often happens when the woman has just served, for the simple reason that she naturally follows through with a step or two after her serve to cover a possible drop, and then, seeing the half court, is tempted to reach back to hit it. Unless she moves *directly* sideways to the alley after her serve in anticipation of the half court, she should *not* touch the bird; she should let it go for her partner to cope with. She will soon realize that, of the two probable returns by her opponents, the half court rather than the drop will usually be their reply when her partner is serving. Since they will prefer a drop when she serves, this is not the time to go for the half courts.

9. There is one problem which must be resolved even though it does not come up too often. This occurs when an opponent has placed a drop shot *very* close to the net, within three or four inches. Is it better to re-drop, even with the woman right there, or take your chances with a clear? If it can be contacted within six inches of net level you do have a choice. You can still clear it quite deep or you can re-drop. Below that point you would *have* to re-drop because any clear you could make would be very short. Of course, the farther the bird is from the net, toward you, the lower you can contact it and still clear it deep.

However, under most circumstances it is better to re-drop. The odds are greatly in your opponents' favor if you clear. Unless you contact the bird close to net level and can use the undercut drop, it is usually better to crosscourt your drop away from the opposing woman who is right there.

10. In net play the woman *should* excel. To make her net play more effective, it would be wise for her to cultivate that excellent stroke: the undercut drop (described under "The Netman's Role," Chapter 4, P. 34). The tumbling and spinning action of the bird makes it too risky to hit until it has righted itself below the net. Another excellent stroke for the woman to learn is used when the opposing man has hit a half court that is neither perfect nor poor (i.e., one that the woman might miss if she tried a drive or a "kill"). She should use a full sweeping motion of the arm as if to drive at the man. This full arm action usually immobilizes *both* opponents momentarily. On contact, however, the bird is sliced by an under-cutting motion of the wrist and so it falls just over the net. This stroke does not have to be played too close to the net; by the time either opponent recovers from the surprise, the bird will be considerably *below* net level and, barring a lucky return, it should be put away on the next hit.

11. One situation that can be troublesome is deciding how to deal with a man who is a particularly effective rusher of both of your serves. First, of course, *try* not to let his tactics affect your serve. Remember that when he makes an error or two which result in outright points for your team, he will not be so likely to continue this aggressiveness. If this fails then try serving to the outside alley with an exaggerated arm movement and with a sideward slicing motion. Even though this kind of serve opens up your court for more angled returns, your arm movement usually keeps him back until the bird is below the net. This gives you a chance to at least get the bird in play.

How you return his punch depends upon where his partner goes. If she backs up to cover a crosscourt drive, your best return is to drive deep over his head, not to her. A drop is risky for as you hit his punch you usually are either cramped or reaching and off balance. Generally you have time only to snap your wrist at the bird and this action works better with a drive or clear than a drop.

If he is the type who punches and then falls back to cover the back area while the woman stays up, a drive to the alley away from him is your best reply.

12. Playing against a strictly sides mixed team can pose a problem if the man does not know how to deal with the situation. It can really be very simple, however, if the man can disguise his drop and smash so that the opposing woman cannot tell which of the two is coming. He must be willing to smash as many times as is required of him throughout the match and be able to do so without making many errors. When the opposing team is back in the sides position, you and your partner need only to drop. The man then follows the general rules for smashing while his partner plays a little farther back than usual to cut off weak returns and to cut off crosscourt drive returns if his smash becomes a little too flat. The inexperienced player makes the mistake of allowing himself to get into a driving game with the opposing woman. This is not the proper strategy to follow when she has only half of the court sideways to cover and you must cover the whole width of the court.

It is difficult to play against a team that plays conventionally part of the time and sides at other times. When the play is fast, switching from one style of play to the other can be very disconcerting if the man is not aware of the situations in which such a change is likely to be made. The usual switch from a conventional formation is made when, with the opposing woman up, the man is forced to hit a fairly defensive shot, or when the opposing woman backs up to cover a crosscourt drive which she feels that her partner will not be able to handle. The temptation here is to drive to the alley away from the man because you know that he is out of position. However the best shot to make is a quick, sliced crosscourt or drop. Perhaps your partner has done a fine job of disguising her drop and your opponents would rather clear than risk a re-drop with her ready for it. Regardless of the situation, the *key* shot here is a drop or at least a downward shot so that you can take the offense on their next return. Then it is simply a matter of the man mixing drops with his smashes to the opposing woman until the point is won by the smash or by your partner at the net. One word of caution to the man: The opposing woman will make every effort to crosscourt her clears; this means that if you smash at her, you will be forced to violate one of the basic rules of smashing (i.e., smashing at the opponent straight ahead). You can get away with crosscourting your smash, however, *if* you make sure that your smash goes all the way over to the alley and that it is well angled downward. Whenever this is not possible, then drop to her side of the middle rather than smash. Another method which allows you to get in front of her so you *can* smash straight ahead is to use a controlled, well-angled, half speed smash to her inside rather than to the alley, thus forcing her to hit her return straight ahead. You then move over and you are where you want to be.

13. As in all doubles play, you must help each other by calling "out" or "no" to shots that are going out. The man can help when the woman is receiving a drive or flick serve. There is one situation peculiar to mixed doubles when the woman can be very helpful and that is when the man is receiving a low serve. She is in perfect position to warn him when the serve is short of the front service line.

5

Frequently
Misunderstood Rules

Knowledge of all the rules is vital if you are to play a game effectively on an advanced level. All players should of course own and study a copy of the *Official Rules,* published by the American Badminton Association. The following are some of the little known and least understood rules. If you are well informed, your knowledge can prevent you from losing unnecessary points.

1. The most controversial are the wood shot and carry rules. Through the years, wood shots have alternated between being legal and a fault. Carrying the bird on the racket, or slinging it, has always been a fault. The latest ruling of the International Badminton Federation states: "It is a fault if the shuttle be held on the racket (i.e., caught or slung) during the execution of a stroke; or if the shuttle be hit twice in succession by the same player with two strokes; or if the shuttle be hit by a player and his partner successively." This rule makes both the wood shot and the so-called double hit legal if they are hit with *one* stroke. An umpire's judgment still must be made regarding what constitutes a sling. However, this latest ruling simplifies the umpire's job considerably. It will tend to lengthen rallies and will reduce the number of situations that cause hard feelings.

2. Most courts do not have a line directly below the net from post to post; such a line would make a distinct division between the court. You may get into the bad habit of going into your opponent's court with one foot on close net shots. Invasion of your opponent's court is a fault while the bird is in play.

3. Related to the above rule are two other situations which it will be to your benefit to know about. When the bird hits the floor, or when it hits the net and obviously is not coming over, play for that rally is over (i.e., the bird is "dead"). Therefore, on your follow-through of a "kill" which is close to the net, should you hit the net with your racket *after* the bird has hit the

floor, you have *not* made a fault. The hitter is given the benefit in any doubtful cases.

In the same category, should you hit the net *after* it has been determined that your opponent's drop shot has hit the net and is not coming over, you have not committed a fault.

4. During play, you may contact birds only when they are on your side of the net. However, you may follow-through across the net *after* contact. Uninformed players will drop shot a bird that is close to the net rather than "kill" it, for fear they will be called by the umpire for "reaching over" on the follow-through.

5. Sometimes a racket is dropped during play. If your opponent's racket goes into your court, he has faulted. If the racket lands in one's own court, play should continue as usual. The natural reaction of course, is to stop play when this happens.

6. You may not make any movement with your racket or body which is meant to distract your opponent when he is in the act of hitting the bird. This rule is most commonly broken when one player has hit a drop shot higher than he intended and when both players are at the net. In this situation, a player cannot place his racket up to the bird so that he blocks his opponent's return (even though he keeps his racket on his own side of the net). He may, however, put his racket up to protect his face.

7. Sometimes as you release the bird on service it will stick to your fingers slightly. When this happens, don't attempt to hit it. If you do, you run the risk of missing your serve because the bird may wobble as you contact it. Let it drop to the floor and try again. There is no penalty for doing this. In fact there is no penalty for stroking at the bird so long as you make no contact with it. Do not think you *have* to attempt to hit the bird on your service even if you release it.

Index

914306